D0949296

Cross-Country Ski Tours

of Washington's South Cascades and Olympics

Tom Kirkendall & Vicky Spring

The Mountaineers • Seattle

THE MOUNTAINEERS: Organized 1906 ". . . to explore, study, preserve and enjoy the natural beauty of the Northwest."

Published by The Mountaineers
306 2nd Ave. W., Seattle, Washington 98119

Published simultaneously in Canada by Douglas & McIntyre, Ltd.
1615 Venables Street, Vancouver, British Columbia V5L 2H1

Edited by Andy Dappen
Copyedited by Nick Allison
Book layout by Ray Weisgerber
Cover designed by Judy Petry
Maps by Tom Kirkendall
Cover photo: Keechelus Lake from Amabilis Mountain (Tour 54)

Photos by the authors
Printed in the United States of America

Library of Congress Cataloging in Publication Data

Kirkendall, Tom.
    Cross-country ski tours of Washington's south Cascades and
Olympics / Tom Kirkendall & Vicky Spring.
        p.   cm.
    Includes index.
    ISBN 0-89886-176-4 (pbk.) :
    1. Cross-country skiing--Washington (State)--Olympic Mountains-
-Guide-books.   2. Cross-country skiing--Cascade Range--Guide-books.
3. Olympic Mountains (Wash.)--Description and travel--Guide-books.
4. Cascade Range--Description and travel--Guide-books.   I. Spring,
Vicky, 1953-   . II. Title.
GV854.5.W33K567 1988
917.97'5--dc19
                                                                    88-8226
                                                                      CIP

2 1 0 9
5 4 3 2

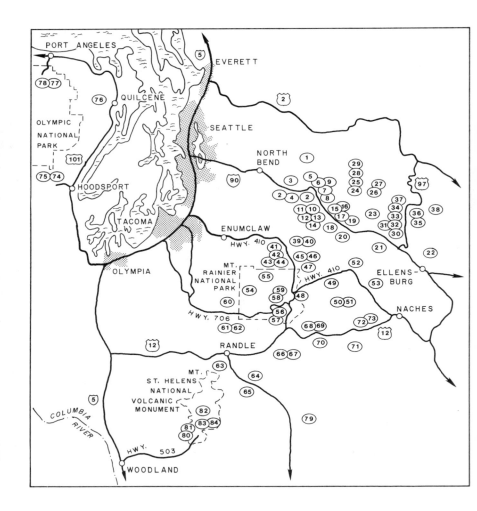

A NOTE ABOUT SAFETY

Cross-country skiing entails unavoidable risks, which every skier must assume. The listing of a route in this book does not guarantee it will be safe for anyone, at any time. Routes vary greatly in difficulty, and skiers vary greatly in skill and physical conditioning. Routes may have changed or conditions deteriorated since the descriptions were written. Also, conditions can change from day to day and even hour to hour, owing to weather and other factors.

Cross-country skiers can minimize the risks on a tour by being knowledgeable, prepared and alert. This book is not designed to fully prepare a skier for all problems encountered when skiing. Many good books are available on the subjects of wilderness survival, first aid, and equipment maintenance; consult one of them for information on these subjects.

It's important for all skiers to recognize their own limitations. Look ahead. If adverse conditions are stacking up against your skill and conditioning, abandon the trip.

CONTENTS

PREFACE
GUARANTEEING OUR WINTER WONDERLAND

Our winter wonderland does not come with a guarantee. Just because you enjoyed a tour up a quiet valley one year does not guarantee it will remain machine-free in the future. Just because there was a Sno-Park at the start of a tour one year does not guarantee parking there the next year. And even though you took the entire Scout troop for an affordable tour this year, you may have to pay a fee to ski in the same place next year.

These examples refer to problems faced by skiers in the last few years. Skiers opened up the old highway between Lake Easton and the Cabin Creek Sno-Park only to have snowmobilers take over part of the trail. The very popular Gold Creek Sno-Park, the only public parking at Snoqualmie Pass, is being phased out over the next few years as private developers take over the area. And the Mill Creek Sno-Park, just east of Stevens Pass, may be closed to allow private developers to charge a fee for use of the area.

Skiers have few areas in the Cascades they can call their own. The main roads throughout the forests are groomed snowmobile speedways which are noisy, smelly, and unsafe for slow-moving skiers. Although numerically cross-country skiers represent a much larger group than snowmobilers, we are allowed only a fraction of the forest for our own use. To ask that a third of all forest roads be set aside for skiers and other self-propelled users would not be unreasonable.

Whether or not more roads are set aside for nonmotorized winter use is an issue that rests solely with us, the cross-country skiers. It is our responsibility to protect the areas reserved for self-propelled use and work to gain more areas. This is not an easy task for individual skiers to perform. Snowmobilers are a well-organized group with lobbyists, representatives, and a lot of money. Skiers are not.

There *is* a way to get involved in protecting our winter wonderland— *write letters*. Write letters to let the Forest Service and State Parks Commission know that you are interested in self-propelled winter recreation, that you are interested in preserving the areas that are currently reserved for the self-propelled, and that you would like to see more areas set aside for nonmotorized winter recreation. If meeting a snowmobile on your tour spoils your day, write about it. If skiing on a road groomed for snowmobiles is not enjoyable, write about it. If you were buzzed by snowmobiles while eating lunch, write about it. In your letter, note the area in which you were skiing, then briefly describe the incident or why you would have enjoyed the tour more if you hadn't had to share it with snowmobiles.

Here are some important addresses that will help you direct your letters to the correct agencies. Write to the Forest Supervisors:

Baker-Snoqualmie National Forest
1018 First Avenue
Seattle, WA 98104

Okanogan National Forest
Okanogan, WA 98840

Wenatchee National Forest
P.O. Box 811
Wenatchee, WA 98801

Gifford Pinchot National Forest
500 West 12th Street
Vancouver, WA 98660

Olympic National Forest
Federal Building
Olympia, WA 98501

If you wish to write regarding the state parks, the address is:

Office of Winter Recreation
Washington State Parks
7150 Cleanwater Lane KY-11
Olympia, WA 98504

As no publication dealing with skiers' concerns exists, we find *Signpost Magazine* to be the best means available for passing information, sharing concerns, initiating letter-writing campaigns, and communicating with other skiers. Subscriptions can be obtained by writing to *Signpost*, 1305 Fourth Avenue, Suite B, Seattle, WA 98101.

Guaranteeing our winter wonderland will not be a quick or an easy process. But if the Forest Service and the Parks Department know that we skiers are concerned with protecting and expanding our access into the forests and that any action depriving us of this very limited resource will be answered by a flood of protest, we will have gone a long way toward writing our own guarantee.

(90) INTERSTATE FREEWAYS		(34) SKI TOUR NUMBER	
(2) U.S. HIGHWAYS		✹ AVALANCHE HAZARD	
(20) STATE HIGHWAYS		⌂ LODGE	
[121] SPUR FOREST ROADS		⊓ HUT	
[67] MAINLINE FOREST ROADS			
DRIVING ROADS		SKIING ROADS	
SKI LIFT		SKIING TRAILS	

INTRODUCTION

Every year more and more people head into the woods on nordic skis. Many are reformed downhillers fleeing from high prices, long lift lines, packed runs, and yodeling on the loudspeaker. Others are ski mountaineers seeking a less strenuous way to spend the winter. Some never have skied at all because neither of the other two forms of the sport appealed to them. Nordic, or cross-country, skiing is something completely different. Anyone can enjoy it—except, perhaps, people who absolutely despise snow.

Washington's Cascade and Olympic Mountains provide infinite opportunity for excellent nordic skiing, whether on groomed trails along peaceful valley floors, on scenic logging roads, or on open slopes of dormant volcanoes that cry out to be telemarked. This book can only begin to suggest how much there is to do and in how many areas. Particular emphasis has been given the needs of the beginning (basic) and intermediate skier who is just learning the country, but trails and routes have been included that will test the advanced and challenge the mountaineer.

To repeat the caution that any guidebook must offer—especially one that deals in so undependable a substance as snow—the reader must keep in mind the publication date of this book. If he skis onto the scene a couple of years later, he must understand that the authors have no control over (1) the building of new roads or washing out of old ones, (2) the rules and regulations of government agencies, and (3) the falling down of trees and the piling up (or not piling up) of snow. In a word: Conditions are never the same twice, so be flexible in your plans.

GUIDE TO THE GUIDEBOOK

User Designation

In order to help you choose a tour we have noted three different user classifications in the Appendix as follows:

Groomed Ski Trail: These are trails with machine-made tracks for skiers and are generally only found at resorts. There will be no machines, dogs, or avalanche dangers on these trails and you should expect to pay for their use.

Self-Propelled: These are areas closed to snowmobiles. You may have the company of snowshoers and hikers on your tour.

Multiple Use: These are tours on roads or trails that must be shared with snowmobiles and four-wheel drivers.

Skill Level

Each of the tours has been classified by the minimum skill required for an enjoyable trip. For the sake of simplicity we have used five levels that are broad and somewhat overlapping; consider them to be merely suggestions.

Basic: No skill requirement. Anyone can have fun the very first time on skis. These tours generally are in open meadows, or valley bottoms, or on level logging roads.

Advanced Basic: The minimum skills required are good balance, kick-glide, and simple stopping techniques such as pole dragging, snowplow, and sitting down—and a good sense of humor. The tours at this level are generally on logging roads, marked Forest Service loops, or prepared tracks.

Intermediate: Tours at this level may be long, steep, or both. Intermediate-level skiers should have endurance and the ability to descend steep slopes in all types of snow conditions. Required skills include the kick-turn, herringbone, traverse, and snowplow turn. Tours at this level are generally on narrow, steep logging roads and may have optional off-road side trips and descent routes.

Advanced: The minimum skills at this level are full control of skis at all times, mastery of the telemark or any turn, and the ability to stop quickly. Some advanced tours require basic routefinding. Trails at this level include summer hiking trails and backcountry routes.

Mountaineer: The minimum skills required in addition to an advanced skill level are competence in routefinding and knowledge of snow and avalanche conditions, glacier travel, weather, winter camping, winter survival, and mountaineering.

Trip Length (X miles to a scenic place)

Snow levels vary from year to year and from day to day and therefore the starting point, especially on logging roads, may vary. A base point (which may or may not be your actual starting point) has been assigned; the trailhead elevation and skiing time are figured from this point.

Skiing Time

This is the time spent skiing to and from the destination and does not include lunch or rest stops. The times are calculated from the trail's base point. If the snowline is above this point, plan less time; if below, plan more. The times given for each trail assume good conditions. If a track must be broken through heavy snow or the surface is extremely hard ice, add a generous amount of extra time.

Variable Miles and Times

In some cases the number of miles and amount of skiing time given are variable. These trails are generally over logging roads where snow level suggests different starting points and destinations in winter and spring.

Best Skiing Time

If you want to know what an "average" snow year is in Washington's Cascade or Olympic Mountains, don't ask a seasoned skier; all you'll get is a year-by-year description of the differences. There never is, in real life, an "average" winter. Some years skiing must be done at 5000 feet or above; other years skiing is good through June at 3000 feet; some years the skiing is superb on Seattle's golf courses for most of January. In an attempt to say when skiing is best for each trail, certain generalizations have been made about that mythical average snow year. The time band given is a narrow one. Skiing often starts as much as a month before given times and lasts a month after. Some winters skiing may not be possible on trails below 4000 to 5000 feet. If in doubt, call the area ranger station, listen to pass reports, or contact local mountain shops before starting out.

Avalanche Potential

Tours in this book have been selected for their safety in winter and no known areas of extreme hazard have been included. The warnings given here are about areas to avoid at times when the snow is unstable. To know when these times are, skiers must make it their responsibility to inform themselves about current weather and snow conditions. The best source for up-to-date information on the weather and avalanche conditions in the Washington Cascades and Olympics is a weather radio with continuous reports from NOAA (National Oceanic and Atmospheric Administration). For specific tours call the ranger station in that district; on weekends there will be a recorded message.

Your best defense against avalanches is knowledge. Check "Suggested Reading" for detailed discussions. Several things to particularly watch for:

• Avalanche danger is especially high *during warming trends or after a heavy snowfall;* at these times avoid leeward slopes and travel on ridge tops.

• Steep hillsides, particularly north-facing, receive their first dose of sun for many months in the spring. After being stable all winter, these slopes may be covered by *spring,* or *climax, avalanches.*

• Wind causes snow to build up on the leeward side of ridges, creating dangerous overhangs called *cornices.* Use caution when approaching a ridge top—you may walk out atop a cornice with empty air beneath. A good rule is never to ski beyond the line of trees or snowblown rocks that mark the true crest of a ridge. It is equally dangerous to ski under a cornice as over it. Cornices may break off and trigger avalanches below.

Forecasting agencies express the daily hazard in the following four classifications:

1. Low Avalanche Hazard—mostly stable snow.
2. Moderate Avalanche Hazard—areas of unstable snow on steep, open slopes or gullies.
3. High Avalanche Hazard—snow pack very unstable. Avalanches highly probable on steep slopes and in gullies.
4. Extreme Avalanche Hazard—travel in the mountains unsafe. Better to head for the beach.

These classifications of *hazard* have to do with the *weather's* contribution to the avalanches. Each trail in this book has been rated as to the *potential* of the *terrain* for avalanches. The two factors of hazard and potential must be put together by the skier to make an accurate judgment of the situation.

If the avalanche potential for the trail is listed as *none*, the trail may be safely skied on days when the hazard is low, moderate, or high.

Areas with *low* avalanche potential normally may be skied on days when the hazard is low or moderate.

A *moderate* avalanche potential indicates the area is always to be skied with caution and then only when the hazard is low.

Avalanche forecasting is not an exact science. As when driving a car, one has to accept a certain amount of risk and use the forecast as a guide, not as a certainty. It is important always to seek up-to-date avalanche information before each trip even for trips of low to moderate avalanche potential.

Maps

Blankets of snow add new difficulties to routefinding. Signs are covered, road junctions are obscured and trails blend into the surrounding countryside. Never start out without a good map of the area to be skied.

To help you find the best map for your tour, we have recommended a topographic map (USGS, Green Trails or both) in the description of each trip. The USGS maps are published by the U.S. Geological Survey. These maps cover the entire country and are unequaled for off-road and off-trail routefinding. Unfortunately, USGS maps are not kept up-to-date in terms of roads and trails. The Green Trails maps are published in Washington and regularly updated; however, these maps do not cover areas beyond the heartland of the Cascades and Olympics.

Both the USGS and Green Trails maps are available at outdoor equipment stores and many Forest Service ranger stations. Another excellent resource is an up-to-date Forest Service Recreation Map, available for a small fee at ranger stations (on weekdays) or by writing the district offices.

Sno-Parks

Sno-Parks are designated winter parking areas plowed throughout the winter for recreationists. Permits are required to park in these areas and the fees provide funds to keep the parking sites open. Cars parking without permits can count on a ticket and possible towing.

Permits are available at outdoor equipment stores or by mail from:

Office of Winter Recreation
Washington State Parks and Recreation Commission
7150 Cleanwater Lane KY-11
Olympia, Washington 98505
Phone: (206) 754-1250

Snow-Play Areas

As the name suggests, these are areas to enjoy the snow by walking, sledding, snowshoeing, skiing, or any other nonmotorized activity. They are great for families and are usually located only a short way from the car. A few require a Sno-Park permit, but most are plowed out by the Forest Service. For specific location contact a ranger station.

HEADING OUT INTO WINTER

This book doesn't explain *how* to ski, just *where*. However, some tips are offered to help orient skiers toward wintertime fun. Further information can be found in "Suggested Reading."

Technique

Cross-country (or nordic) skiing looks simple enough, but proper technique is very important to ensure a good time. Even expert downhillers have problems the first day on nordic skis. The narrowness, flexible bindings, and low shoes give an entirely different feeling. Books are helpful, but one or two lessons may be needed. Many organizations offer a two-lesson plan, the first to get you started in the right direction and the second to correct any problems you have.

Clothing

There is no dress code for cross-country skiing. Clothing can be anything from high-fashion Lycra® to mismatched army surplus. However, many of the garments sold for cross-country skiing are designed for resort skiing or racing, providing flexibility and style, but not much warmth.

In the wilderness, warmth is crucial. Covering your body from head to toe in wool or polypropylene, using two or more layers on the upper body to regulate heating, ensures a pleasant journey rather than a bone-chilling ordeal. So go ahead and wear that designer outfit, but be sure and have a layer of long underwear on underneath and another layer with you that can be put on over it.

Rain gear is essential. A poncho keeps snow and rain off a person who is standing still, but can be somewhat awkward when one is skiing. Rain pants and jackets made of coated nylon or breathable waterproof material work best for warmth, dryness, and flexibility.

Skis and Boots

What length of ski to buy, with side cut or without, with metal edges or without, hard or soft camber? What boots are best, high- or low-topped? These and many more questions could fill a book—and they do. Our one and only suggestion is to purchase a waxless ski as your first pair.

Learning to ski can be complicated enough without the frustration of trying to wax for the ever-changing snow conditions. When looking for that new pair of skis, avoid stores that just happen to have a few cross-country skis in stock. Stores that have special cross-country departments and employees who enjoy cross-country skiing will be able to give you a better understanding of what you need and what you don't.

Cross-country boots come in two varieties, lightweight and flexible for track skiing and light touring, and heavyweight with lug soles for backcountry and telemark skiing. The type of boots you have will determine the type of bindings you need, so buy the boots first.

What to Take

Every skier who ventures into the wilderness should be prepared to spend the night out. Winter storms can come with great speed and force, creating whiteouts that leave the skier with nowhere to go. Each ski pack must include the ten essentials, plus one:

1. Extra clothing—more than needed in the worst of weather.
2. Extra food—there should be some left over at the end of the trip.
3. Sunglasses—a few hours of bright sun on snow can cause a pounding headache or temporary blindness.
4. Knife—for first aid and emergency repairs.
5. First-aid kit—just in case.
6. Fire starter—chemical starter to get wet wood burning.
7. Matches in a waterproof container—to start a fire.
8. Flashlight—be sure to have extra batteries with bulb.
9. Map—make sure it's the right one for the trip.
10. Compass—keep in mind the declination.

Plus 1: Repair kit—including a spare ski tip, spare screws and binding bail (if changeable), heavy-duty tape, a few feet of braided picture wire and heavy string, and a combination wrench-pliers-screwdriver.

Other items to carry may include a small shovel, sun cream, and a large plastic tarp to use as a "picnic blanket" or for emergency shelter. All these items should fit comfortably into a day pack. Obviously, a fanny pack will not hold all the items listed above. Fanny packs are strictly for track and resort skiing where one is carrying only a sandwich and a few waxes.

Winter Camping

Most campgrounds are closed in winter by snow. However, some state parks remain open, with plowed access roads and one or two campsites and offering the added attraction of heated restrooms.

When winter camping takes you out into wilderness, camp wherever you feel safe. Avoid pitching a tent under trees heavy with snow; when least expected (day or night), "mushrooms" may fall from above and crush your tent.

Whether in the backcountry or on groomed tracks of a resort, carry out your garbage. (If you packed it in full, you can pack it out empty.) Burying leftovers under a few inches of snow only hides them until the spring melt. Also be careful with human waste. Hidden beneath the snow may be a stream or a summer hiking trail.

Water can be difficult to come by in winter. Most small streams are either hidden beneath the snow or flowing in grand white canyons too steep to descend. If day-skiing, carry water. On a trip lasting overnight or longer, carry a long string for lowering a bucket to an open stream as well as a stove and enough fuel to melt snow. Even in winter, the water from streams in areas where people and/or beavers and other such critters live in summer should be boiled or chemically purified.

When spending the day or several days out skiing, take care where you park your car. A sudden winter storm can make bare and dry logging roads deep in white and impossible to drive, leaving your car stranded— maybe until the spring melt. Always travel with a shovel in the car and a watchful eye on the weather.

Pets

Although in some jurisdictions the family pet is permitted to tag along on summer hikes, wintertime should be left to the two-legged family members. Skiing through knee-deep powder is lots of fun, but not for the ski-less family pet, floundering in a white morass. Pets also tend to destroy ski tracks by leaving behind deep paw prints and brown klister.

Multiple-Use

Until more areas can be designated skier-only, sharing the way with snowshoers, snowmobilers, dog sleds, and four-wheel drivers will have to be tolerated. However, multiple-use is not totally impossible. For example, in the Methow Valley snowmobilers and skiers understand and respect each other's rights and needs. The snowmobilers know the difference between their machines, which destroy ski trails, and the mechanical ski-tracking machines, which create grooves for skis. In exchange for the snowmobilers' courtesy, skiers make their tracks on the edge of a road, leaving the middle for the speeding machines.

Be Flexible

During research for this book many ranger districts and ski patrols were interviewed and one point was stressed: "Be flexible." Have an alternate, safer trip plan if weather changes to create a high avalanche potential in your favorite area. If your second choice is also unsafe, plan a walk along a beach or to the city park. Your exercise of good judgment will help ranger districts and ski areas avoid the necessity of total winter closure for *all* users in order to protect a few thoughtless ones from their own stupidity.

1 BESSEMER MOUNTAIN

Skill level: intermediate
Round trip: 8 miles
Skiing time: 4–6 hours
Elevation gain: 3800 feet

High point: 5000 feet
Best: January–April
Avalanche potential: low
Map: Green Trails, Mount Si

Ski Bessemer Mountain for the views: broad views west over Puget Sound country to Seattle and the Olympic Mountains; close-up views of the rugged cliffs of Garfield Mountain; and an aerial view of the Middle Fork Snoqualmie River Valley. Most winters the Middle Fork road is snow-free, so except for bathtub-sized chuckholes, there usually is a good chance of driving to the trip start.

Access: Drive Interstate 90 east past North Bend and go off on Exit 34, Edgewick Road. Cross left under the freeway, pass Ken's Truck Town, and turn right on SE Middle Fork Snoqualmie River Road. At 5.2 miles cross the Middle Fork and at 6.8 miles spot a prominent but unmarked road angling up left. Watch carefully because several other unmarked roads go only a short distance. At 1 mile from the Middle Fork Road reach

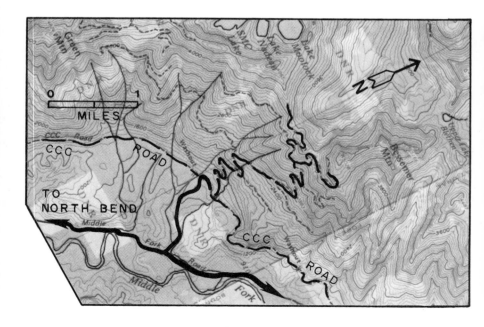

Mount Garfield rising above the Middle Fork Snoqualmie River

the old CCC (Civilian Conservation Corps) Truck Road (1277 feet). This is the base point for the trip, since washouts often halt driving here, or soon after, or even before.

The Tour: Washouts permitting, however, drive to the snowline. Turn right on the CCC Truck Road a scant ¼ mile to an unmarked junction and go left, uphill, in a series of switchbacks that climb relentlessly through tall second-growth forest, then short second-growth, then bare-slope clearcuts. Views are excellent and get steadily bigger and better. At 2000 feet, 1½ miles from the 1277-foot base point, is a well-defined Y, presenting a choice. Let snow conditions make the decision.

The left fork climbs 2½ miles to a 4500-foot knoll atop the Bessemer-Green Ridge with exciting 360-degree views to go with lunch. The grade on this road is relatively gentle, suitable to a day when the snow is icy and a skier might have trouble standing up on a steeper slope.

For an even more gigantic summit view, climb the steeper right fork 2 miles to a 5000-foot flat-top promontory (bulldozed flat by the loggers!), a snowball's throw from the summit of South Bessemer Mountain. One stretch just below the promontory traverses a very steep slope that is perfect for an advanced skier when the snow is deep or sticky, but could be hazardous if icy. In such cases don't try to cross, but be satisfied with the views of the Cascades and assume it would be too hazy anyway to see Puget Sound country on the other side.

2 MILWAUKEE RAILROAD GRADE

West Side

Skill level: basic
Round trip: up to 9 miles
Skiing time: up to 5 hours
Elevation gain: 600 feet
High point: 2160 feet
Best: mid-December–February
Avalanche potential: low
Map: Green Trails, Bandera

East Side

Skill level: basic
Round trip: 4 miles or more
Skiing time: 2 hours or more
Elevation gain: none
High point: 2600 feet
Best: mid-December–April
Avalanche potential: low
Map: Green Trails, Snoqualmie Pass

Perfect beginner's tours are as hard to come by in the Cascades as a winning Lotto ticket, but when parking can be found, one jackpot is the abandoned Milwaukee Railroad Grade. On the west side of Snoqualmie Pass views of the gleaming white slopes of Bandera and Granite mountains abound, antlike cars scurry up and down I-90, and the South Fork of the Snoqualmie River meanders below. On the east side of the pass,

Skiing through an old railroad snowshed along Keechelus Lake

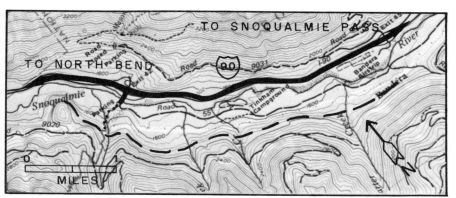

RAILROAD GRADE WEST

RAILROAD GRADE EAST

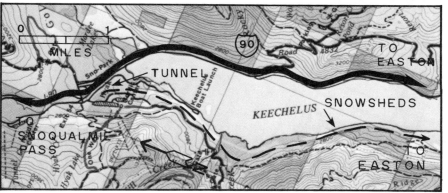

views of Kendall Knob, Keechelus Ridge, and Mount Catherine prevail as the grade carves through forests, clearcuts and along the shores of Keechelus Lake.

The railroad grade provides an almost level ski track and is great for practicing both the long, gliding, diagonal stride of the traditional skier or the high-speed, leg-stretching skate of the nouveau skier.

Although rarely used by the motorized crowd, the railroad grade is currently open to snowmobiles. However, a dedicated group is working on the "Rails To Trails" concept that would close the old railroad grade to motors and create a network of trails spanning the state. (See John Wayne Trail [Tour 21] for details.)

West Side

Access: The west-side railroad grade is reached by following Interstate 90 to Exit 42. Drive southwest, crossing the Snoqualmie River bridge to

Sledge rides on the railroad grade at Snoqualmie Pass

reach the McClellan Butte Trailhead. Generally a plowed parking area exists near the trailhead. If no parking area has been plowed out, ski elsewhere. Do not block the entrance to the highway maintenance shed or the interchange area, or your bank balance will soon diminish and your car may take a trip without you.

The Tour: Starting at 1500 feet, either walk or ski the McClellan Butte foot trail for ½ mile to the abandoned railroad tracks (1800 feet), and a choice. To the right follow the tracks along a very gentle downhill grade about ½ mile to a windswept viewpoint (1720 feet). To the left, east from the trail, ski the grade 4 gentle, uphill miles to the Hansen Creek trestle (2160 feet). The trestle is hazardous to cross and the slopes beyond may avalanche, so turn around here.

East Side

Access: Drive I-90 east from Snoqualmie Pass to Exit 54. Go north to the Gold Creek Sno-Park. (Note: The Gold Creek Sno-Park may soon be closed and cross-country skiers forced to park illegally where they can—(see Tour 6 for more details). As far as alternate parking locations go, on weekdays it is possible to park at Pacific West Ski Area.) As long as the Sno-Park is open, park there and walk back under the freeway and through the ski-area parking lot. Walk to the Pac West lodge, then go down the hill on a beaten trail to the lower parking lot. Go through the lot and straight out the access road to the railroad grade.

The Tour: Once on the railroad grade both directions are musts. To the west, ski ⅛ mile past a cluster of old houses to the Snoqualmie Tunnel. In the winter of 1987 the boards had been torn off the entrance and you could look inside at a wondrous display of cascading flows of ice. Do not venture into the tunnel; these massive flows of ice occasionally collapse, and when they do they'd make a pancake of anyone foolhardy enough to be nearby.

The main tour lies to the east, where you ski along Keechelus Lake. For very young skiers a turnoff on the left in ⅛ mile accesses a road to the lake. The lumps and bumps along the lake's shore can offer kids hours of fun. Skiers remaining on the railroad grade will head back into the trees, cross Mill Creek at 1¼ miles on a solid earth bridge and Cold Creek ¼ mile beyond on a single log. At 2 miles comes the first of two old snow sheds, designed to keep the trains from being swept away in avalanches. On wet days the sheds offer perfect shelter for eating lunch.

It is possible to stay with the railroad grade for miles, going on around the lake to the Stampede Pass Road, although a couple of obstacles exist. The snow sheds are one such obstacle. Usually you must carry your skis through them. The other obstacles are bridges. Some of the wooden bridges have partially collapsed and you should exercise considerable caution when crossing these ruins.

SOUTH FORK SNOQUALMIE RIVER

3 BANDERA OVERLOOK

Skill level: advanced basic
Round trip: 5 miles
Skiing time: 3 hours
Elevation gain: 885 feet

High point: 2485 feet
Best: January–February
Avalanche potential: low
Map: Green Trails, Bandera

When the snow level descends from mountain passes to the lowlands of Puget Sound and roads could serve as championship skating rinks, the Bandera Overlook is usually accessible. The overlook, a flat promontory ideal for lunch and a little early-season sunbathing, stands high above the South Fork Snoqualmie River. From river and freeway and snow-covered valley the eye rises to a skyline of ridges and peaks. When the snow level jumps back up to the lofty heights, there is still good skiing on Mason Lake Way, an alternate road leading to views.

Access: Drive Interstate 90 east from North Bend 14.9 miles and go off on Exit 45, signed "Bandera Airport." Park only in the Sno-Park on the south or north side of the freeway. *Do not* park in the interchange area.

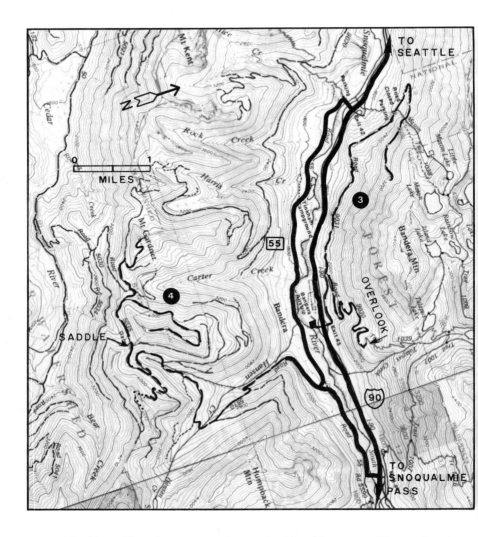

The Tour: The trip starts on the north side of Interstate 90 on a forest road. The first ½ mile parallels the freeway to a major junction. (Straight ahead is Mason Lake Way, which does not go to the lake.) For the overlook bear right on Road 9030.

The road climbs steadily for a mile through heavy forest which opens up to reveal Mount Gardner and a frozen-looking McClellan Butte. At 2 miles Granite Mountain appears to the northeast. Stripped of trees as it is, there would seem to be great skiing on the open slopes, but extremely high avalanche danger makes it a better mountain to just look at.

The main road ends at the overlook. If time remains after trying to

Skiing near Bandera Overlook

name all the peaks and drainages from McClellan Butte to the backside of the Snoqualmie ski areas, continue east another ½ mile. The way becomes brushy and narrow and is skied for fun rather than views.

When the snow level is higher than Interstate 90, drive as far as possible on Mason Lake Way, then ski on up the road to the open slopes under Bandera Mountain, with views rivaling those from the overlook.

Granite Mountain from Hansen Creek Valley

SOUTH FORK SNOQUALMIE RIVER

4 HANSEN CREEK

Skill level: intermediate
Round trip: 2–15 miles
Skiing time: 2–8 hours
Elevation gain: up to 2693 feet
High point: 4693 feet

Best: March–May
Avalanche potential: low
Map: Green Trails, Bandera

Map on page 24

Throughout the winter the Hansen Creek area is inaccessible for all practical purposes, due to the lack of parking and high avalanche potential. In spring, however, there are valleys, ridge tops, clearcuts, and miles of logging roads to explore on skis—and miles and miles of green valleys and white mountains to look at.

Access: Drive Interstate 90 east from North Bend. Go off on Exit 47 and turn right on Asahel Curtis–Tinkham Road for .2 mile to a "T" intersection and the end of pavement. Take the right fork 1.3 miles and turn left on Hansen Creek road No. 5510, which climbs steadily west .8 mile to a wide turnout on the left (2000 feet). Park here or at the snowline.

The Tour: From the parking area the road turns abruptly south, entering Hansen Creek Valley and crossing under a tall, spindly train trestle. At just over one mile pass a spur to the left and, in a long ½ mile more, a second spur. Beyond the second intersection the road levels off in the upper valley and enters clearcuts. Views begin, starting with Bandera Mountain to the north. Stay on the main road as it crosses Hansen Creek at 2 miles (2900 feet), and swings around onto a side valley; Granite Mountain appears, to the east of Bandera. At 3 miles cross an unnamed tributary of Hansen Creek and reach a major junction. Take the left fork, heading up the valley. From this point the choice of objectives should be made by available time and energy.

The saddle at the end of the valley is the closest of many good turnarounds. Follow the road as it curves left around the valley head and take the first right back to the ridge top (3900 feet) at 5½ miles. Gaze southeast over the Cedar River Valley, source of Seattle's water.

From the saddle there are two possibilities, north or south. The south leads to good downhill skiing in clearcuts and on 2 miles to a 4693-foot knoll with views of Rainier, Cedar River, and McClellan Butte. Ski the approach road back ½ mile, then ascend to the top right corner of a large clearcut. A short passage through trees emerges in another clearcut just below the summit.

North from the saddle the road provides views over the South Fork Snoqualmie, from the ribbon-like freeway in the valley up to rugged summits of Snoqualmie Pass peaks. At 1½ miles the road ends in views that include Mount Gardner, Bandera Mountain, and Mount Defiance.

KEECHELUS LAKE

5 SNOQUALMIE PASS— TRACKED AND UNTRACKED

Skill level: basic
Round trip: 8 miles
Skiing time: 4 hours
Elevation gain: 1360 feet

High point: 4000 feet
Best: mid-December–April
Avalanche potential: low
Map: Green Trails, Snoqualmie Pass

Not long ago cross-country skiers were stereotyped as long-haired hippies, smelling of pine tar and wet wool, who used bamboo ski poles that left peace-sign imprints in the snow. Those "granola" skiers used to drive to Snoqualmie Pass, park with the downhill skiers, then head out to the uncharted forest behind the ski areas.

Today the uncharted forests of the pass have been replaced by the maintained trails of two nordic centers—one at Ski Acres and the other at Hyak (Pac West). What was once free now costs you a few bucks (not a bad deal for those in search of groomed trails). The pass is also a marvelous place to witness how modern technology transformed the sport. The granola skier has shed his natural skin for one of plastic. Skis, poles, boots, and even clothing are made from plastic derivatives.

Access: Drive I-90 to Snoqualmie Pass and take Exit 53 to Ski Acres. The Cross-Country Center is located at the far end of the ski area. To reach Hyak, take Exit 54 and drive right into the Pac-West parking area.

The Tracked: The Cross-Country Center at Ski Acres features 20 kilometers (about 12½ miles) of beautifully groomed track which wanders through forest and meadows on relatively level terrain. You'll also find a one-mile loop, four lanes wide (including a skating lane), with lights for night skiing. The area has no avalanche hazard, plenty of room for families and beginners, ski rentals, and lessons. The future looks good for this area, so look for more trails and a lodge in the years to come.

Hyak (Pac West) has been a popular area for cross-country skiing since the skinny skis were first imported from Scandinavia. Fees seem to change with the weather. Some days you'll pay a parking fee, other days only a trail fee.

The trails at Hyak were originally brushed out by volunteers and maintained with the blessing of the Forest Service and the ski area. However, as long as the ski area actively grooms the paths they will charge a trail fee.

The trails are generally groomed for at least 3 miles along the logging roads of Cold Creek. Along the first mile you'll have excellent views over Keechelus Lake followed by several miles of forests and clearcuts. The terrain is mostly level with several short hills for thrills. Don't be afraid to try skiing here even if you've only been on the boards once or twice—the Nordic Patrol monitors the trails, renders assistance as needed, and steers skiers away from potential hazards.

The Untracked: In addition to the groomed trails at Hyak, many marked loops originate at the ski area (see map). The most popular of these loops is the 8-mile tour around Mount Catherine, suitable for intermediate skiers. From the parking lot (2640 feet), climb along the rope tow toward the chalet on the left side of the ski area, to a wide ski trail. Head left following the trail along a logging road, maintaining a constant elevation while traversing east through the timber. After ½ mile a road comes in from the left; continue straight ahead. This trail is usually groomed for 3 miles to the base of a switchback.

The climb begins as the road heads up the switchback and then on up the valley. Several dead-end spurs are passed. Ignore them, sticking to the main road marked by blue diamonds. After 4½ miles the road reaches aptly named Windy Pass (3800 feet). Just beyond the pass, leave the road as it bends to the left and ski down a sloping hill, losing 160 feet of elevation to reach the snow-covered Olallie Meadow. Bear right, across the top

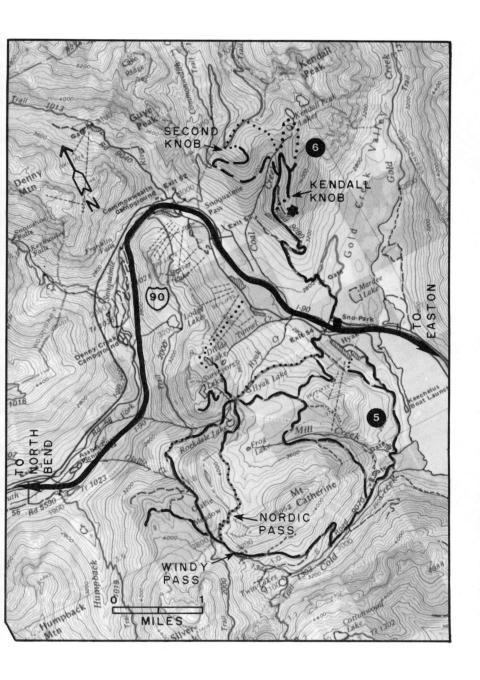

29

Skiers near Three Forks Junction

end of the meadow, then climb steeply to the east for ¼ mile to Nordic Pass (4000 feet).

Staying on the route through dense timber now becomes a challenge. Keep to the left (north) side of the valley to a logging road at 5½ miles (3700 feet). Follow the road to the right around Rockdale Lake to Three Forks Junction. Go right and glide along the top of the ridge to the ski area, at 7½ miles. The final ½-mile descent is on groomed downhill slopes. Follow the cat road down the resort's famous landmark, the giant beer can. Then telemark the main slopes (or continue following the road) down to the parking lot.

KEECHELUS LAKE

6 KENDALL—KNOBS, LAKES, AND LOOPS

Skill level: basic
Round trip: 7 miles
Skiing time: 4 hours
Elevation gain: 1700 feet
High point: 4400 feet

Best: December–April
Avalanche potential: moderate
Map: Green Trails, Snoqualmie Pass

Map on page 29

Open slopes or logging roads, views or small forested lakes, are the options in this versatile area below Kendall Peak at Snoqualmie Pass. Kids can leave their parents on the downhill slopes (or vice versa) and head out for some nordic skiing just across the valley. Arrive early to secure a parking spot and be prepared for a lot of company; this is the only area at the pass where no trail fee is charged for skiing.

The fate of this area is uncertain. Developers intending to build vacation houses in Gold Creek Valley wish to eliminate the Sno-Park and all skier access to the area as early as the winter of 1988 or 1989. At this time there are no plans to open another public Sno-Park at Snoqualmie Pass. We hope that skier outrage will convince the Forest Service and the State Parks Department to find a way to keep this area open or to open another. If you would like to help save public parking at Snoqualmie Pass, please write a letter to the North Bend District Ranger, 42404 SE North Bend Way, North Bend, WA 98045, and to James Horan, Office of Winter Recreation, Washington State Parks, 7150 Cleanwater Lane KY-11, Olympia, WA 98504, stating your desire for a Sno-Park at the pass.

Access: Drive Interstate 90 east from Snoqualmie Pass 2 miles and take Rocky Run Exit No. 54. Park in the Gold Creek Sno-Park on the north side of the freeway along the plowed section of the old highway (2640 feet). (If the Sno-Park is closed, park in the new area or make arrangements with Pac West to park in the resort lot.) From the Sno-Park pick one of four possible destinations.

Skiers on First Kendall Knob

Gold Creek Loops: This is the best choice for novice skiers and the one most certain to be lost when developers start building in the area. Ski north up the Gold Creek Valley on level road. At ⅛ mile the road turns uphill and climbs quite steeply. After ½ mile, the road forks; go right, following the trail of blue diamonds. Now the fun begins. The route follows a rough spur road north, back down to the valley floor. If you have had enough fun, return down the valley on an old spur road that branches off on the right just before you reach the valley floor, making a short loop. The long loop follows a thin trail of blue diamonds across an open plain heading towards Gold Creek. As the route enters the trees it swings south, following a series of narrow roads, and ends in a steep descent to a log-scaling station. Head out to the main road then walk or ski ⅓ mile to the right, back to the starting point.

First Kendall Knob: This tour, suited to intermediate-level skiers, follows the same route as the Gold Creek Loops for the first ½ mile. When the road divides, go left and switchback up through an old clearcut. Two major spur roads are passed, the first on the right and the second on the left, as your road heads into the first of two steep switchbacks. At 2 miles (3600 feet) the road heads north. At first, trees line the uphill side of the road. When these trees end take careful note. A narrow avalanche chute borders the edge of the clearcut; when conditions are unstable turn around here. When conditions are stable continue on up the road until it ends on a flat landing atop the knob (4400 feet).

When the snow pack is stable the slopes between the knob and the road below offer an exhilarating descent route.

Kendall Peak Lakes: The lakes offer a peaceful backcountry escape for advanced skiers as well as an outstanding run down through the trees. Following the First Kendall Knob route, ski 3¾ miles to the narrow saddle on the ridge directly below First Kendall Knob. The road and knob skiers go right; lake skiers go left. Climb up over two short rises, then head left into the trees and traverse north to a stream drainage. Turn uphill and follow the stream to the lowest lake (4300 feet), a short ½ mile from the knob. The second lake lies another ¼ mile up the valley. This is the turnaround point, as serious avalanche hazard lies beyond.

For the return trip, ski straight down the valley from the lakes to intersect the road leading to the knob. Widely spaced trees provide telemarkers with fun obstacles to negotiate and the snow remains powdery long after the exposed slopes turn to mush.

Second Kendall Knob: This 10-mile tour offers two approaches, the best telemarking in the area, and views galore. To the south you'll look over the white blanket covering Keechelus Lake. In the western skies rise Meadow Mountain, Tinkham Peak, and Mount Rainier. Silver Peak, Mount Catherine, and all the ski resorts of Snoqualmie Pass lie right beneath your feet. To the north Guye Peak, Denny Mountain, The Tooth, Bryant Peak, and Chair Peak pierce the sky. And to the east sits the Alpine Lakes Wilderness Area with its enclave of protected trees terminating at the buttresslike walls of Kendall Peak.

Ski up the road to the First Kendall Knob for 3¼ miles. Pass the avalanche chute then cross a clearcut slope to a point where a steep hill rises on the left. Shortly beyond, a road takes off on the right and another on the left. Take the left-hand road, ski across a clearcut, descend slightly, cross Coal Creek, and climb again. The road ends in an open basin near the top. Continue on, breaking your own trail for the final ¼ mile to the summit of the 4720-foot knob.

An alternate approach is to continue past the turnoff to the Second Kendall Knob at 3¼ miles and ski up the main road until it switchbacks. Go left here on an old logging road to its end, then head up and to the left, working your way through the trees. Avoiding all steep slopes, head up toward the ridge top above. Just below the ridge crest find a shelf which is followed south to the edge of the clearcut and the summit of the Second Kendall Knob.

For the descent, the slopes heading due west down from the summit are the most open and stable. The slopes on the south side are steep and rocky and should only be skied in very stable conditions.

7 MOUNT MARGARET

Skill level: intermediate
Round trip: 9 miles to false summit
Skiing time: 5 hours
Elevation gain: 2880 feet

High point: 5440 feet
Best: January–mid-April
Avalanche potential: moderate
Map: Green Trails, Snoqualmie Pass

The west side of Mount Margaret offers open slopes that compare to the best downhill ski areas in length and variety. A day may be spent making challenging runs down the clearcut hillside or climbing to the rugged ridge just below the summit of Mount Margaret to enjoy the extraordinary views.

Do not ski this tour after a heavy snowfall or rainstorm. Before the west side of the mountain was completely logged, Mount Margaret was considered a safe area for touring in almost any conditions. Now, with over 2000 vertical feet of barren slopes, the section of this tour paralleling the freeway is potentially dangerous.

Access: Drive Interstate 90 east from Snoqualmie Pass 2 miles to Rocky Run Exit 54. Go under the freeway to the north side and turn right at the Gold Creek Sno-Park. Drive .8 mile and park near the end of the plowed

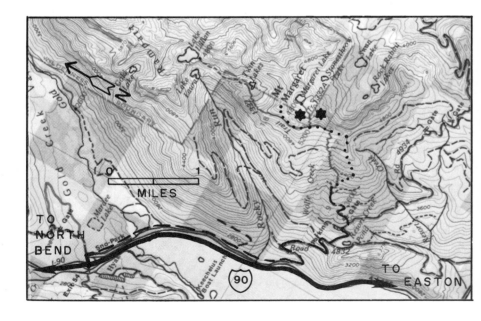

Lunch on the false summit of Mount Margaret, Mount Rainier in distance

road (2560 feet). This is still part of the Sno-Park area so be sure to have a permit.

The Tour: The first section parallels the freeway east along Keechelus Lake for 2 miles. After passing several summer homes, the road turns uphill into timber and sets about the serious business of gaining elevation.

Near the end of the first mile of climbing, the road enters open clearcuts. Skiers may choose either to stay on the road or to leave it and strike out over the rolling slopes. An abrupt switchback at 3 miles is the scene of a possibly confusing intersection; stay right. At 3½ miles is another junction. The right fork descends gradually 6 miles to the Kachess Lake road. Take the left fork and climb steeply. Pass the summer parking lot for the Mount Margaret–Lake Lillian Trail (3600 feet). After another 100 yards take a spur road on the left and head steeply uphill, following the summer route to Mount Margaret. Once over the initial steep climb look up to the top of the clearcuts above. The objective is to reach the upper right corner either on the road or across the slopes and not be totally distracted by the terrific views, dominated by Mount Rainier and Keechelus Lake.

From the top of the clearcut follow a logging road to a higher clearcut. Continue on the road to the upper left corner and through a narrow band of trees overlooked by the loggers to a final clearcut and the road-end. Climb past ghost trees to the ridge top (4800 feet), where whole new horizons extend south over miles of logged slopes to the Stampede Pass area. Intermediate-level skiers should turn around here.

The rest of the climb is in timber. Follow the crest when the going is easy, and drop a bit on the west side when the ridge is rough. Stay well away from the edge—the east side often is corniced and it's a long drop to the bottom. Several places give views to the summit and false summit.

The final ascent is up partially open slopes to the 5440-foot false summit. Taking care to stay well back from the corniced edge, gaze to the dark granite massif of Mount Stuart. Bears Breast Mountain stands out among Dutch Miller Gap peaks. West and north are spiky peaks near Snoqualmie Pass.

The summit of Mount Margaret lies temptingly near, but the views don't improve with the 90 extra feet of elevation and the route crosses steep slopes and giant cornices. It's best left as an excuse to return in summer.

The descent may be made by heading down through the trees below the false summit, then down through the clearcuts all the way to Interstate 90.

YAKIMA RIVER

8 FLATLANDERS' ROUTE ON KEECHELUS RIDGE

Skill level: basic
Round trip: up to 8 miles
Skiing time: up to 4 hours
Elevation gain: 900 feet

High point: 3380 feet
Best: December–March
Avalanche potential: low
Map: Green Trails, Snoqualmie Pass

Grunting up a steep hill isn't necessary in order to gain a fine view of the Keechelus Lake area. A forested road paralleling Interstate 90 provides excellent touring with only minor elevation gain and several clearcuts for practicing climbing and descending skills. If mingling with snowmobiles isn't your idea of a good time, ski the road during midweek.

Access: West-siders, drive 10 miles east of Snoqualmie Pass to the Stampede Pass Exit No. 62. Turn left, cross the overpass, and return to

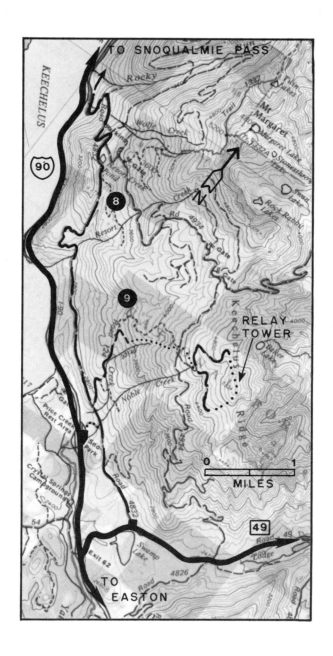

View over Keechelus Lake and surrounding hills

the freeway heading west. Drive 1 mile to the westbound Price Creek Sno-Park Rest Area. East-siders will find the Sno-Park 1 mile past the Stampede Pass exit. For the return trip, however, you will have to drive 7 miles west to the Hyak–Rocky Run Exit 54 before making the U-turn east.

The Tour: At the west end of the Sno-Park find the combined ski-snowmobile trail, which climbs up to a clearcut. Here the trail divides; snowmobilers veer right while skiers and maverick snowmobilers head left. Cross two creeks, one of which is Price Creek.

At ⅛ mile turn right on Forest Road (4832)125, unsigned here, and climb steeply for several hundred feet to wide Forest Road 4832. Turn left. The road continues climbing, but anyone feeling their iron deficiency will take comfort in knowing the steepest part of the tour lies behind. Now comes the payoff, with a chance to walk, cruise, glide, skate, or enjoy views. The first viewpoint is a short ¼ mile farther on, overlooking Keechelus Lake Dam and up Meadow Creek Valley.

Glide along the base of a clearcut, then cross Resort Creek at the 2-mile mark (2800 feet). Climb away from Keechelus Lake over a 3380-foot saddle to Resort Creek Pond (3300 feet), a good turning point.

If transportation can be arranged, follow Road 4832 for 3 additional miles to Gold Creek at the south end of the Rocky Run Sno-Park. The last 2 miles to the Sno-Park parallel Interstate 90 and it isn't quite like Fifth Avenue in New York, but it is noisy. You might consider pulling out the Walkman and cranking up the tunes—even a heavy-metal band beats the racket of the eighteen-wheelers.

9 RELAY TOWER–KEECHELUS RIDGE

Skill level: advanced
Round trip: 6 miles
Skiing time: 4 hours
Elevation gain: 2120 feet
High point: 4960 feet

Best: December–April
Avalanche potential: low
Map: Green Trails, Snoqualmie Pass

Map on page 37

If telemarking is your addiction, one of the best midwinter fixes in the Snoqualmie Pass area is found on the clearcut hillsides of Keechelus Ridge. Excellent views of most of the major peaks around Snoqualmie Pass also distinguish this tour.

Access: Drive to the westbound Price Creek Sno-Park/Rest Area as described in Tour 8.

The Tour: Following the signed ski route from the Sno-Park, climb to Forest Road 4832. Turn left for 30 feet, then right on Road (4832)124 for the climb. Ski along the upper edge of a clearcut and round a crew-cut hill with Price Creek on the right. As the hill on the left comes to an end you'll find an unmarked and somewhat confusing intersection (slightly over ½ mile from the Sno-Park). Take the narrow and somewhat overgrown road on the far right and trudge steeply uphill.

View northwest from Keechelus Ridge

The road climbs south while Price Creek swings southeast. At 1 mile watch for another abandoned road branching right and follow it back toward Price Creek. When the creek becomes visible turn uphill, following a steep cat track and the creek. Switchback up to a small bench, then another, and then another. The creek disappears and the big disappointment appears—what looked like the hilltop from below is just another bench.

Continue up, crossing Road (4834)124 and Road 4934 (4320 feet). In 1986 a heavy band of trees towered straight above. If the timber recession has saved them, use the trees as a guide and contour around to the right then on up. If the chainsaw murderers have paid a visit, just head straight up. The relay tower comes into view at the crest of the next ridge. The tower is reached at 3 miles (4960 feet) and it's a good point to take in the view. Mount Rainier hovers above the southern forests while Mount Stuart dominates the eastern horizon. In between you'll find Mount Margaret, Rampart Ridge, Box Ridge, Denny Mountain, Mount Catherine, Silver Peak, and more. Better pull out the map and learn all the bumps if you want to impress the next person you drag up here.

If following your tracks back sounds tame, head north along the ridge top to a long, narrow saddle, then head down. The telemark run through a narrow band of trees and clearcuts will pump the adrenalin. Continue skiing straight down until you reach your uphill tracks.

YAKIMA RIVER

10 THAT DAM LOOP

Skill level: *advanced basic*
Round trip: *5 miles*
Skiing time: *3 hours*
Elevation gain: *80 feet*

High point: *2480 feet*
Best: *mid-December–February*
Avalanche potential: *none*
Map: *Green Trails, Snoqualmie Pass*

Loops are fun and this one is no exception. Wind through forest, cross a snow-laced stream, skim over the Yakima River, and ski across the Keechelus Lake Dam on a trail perched at the very top.

A word of caution. This is a shared trail so watch your fanny. The Forest Service does not regulate the speed or direction of snowmobiles on such trails because the public has not yet asked for it. Be courteous to snowmobilers, and if they give you cause for complaint, contact the Forest Service immediately. Registration numbers or automobile license plates may be helpful, so if problems occur, be a hero—let the Forest Service know.

Access: Drive Interstate 90 east from Snowqualmie Pass 9.1 miles to the eastbound Price Creek Sno-Park/Rest Area. (Westbound traffic must go to Exit 54 and return.)

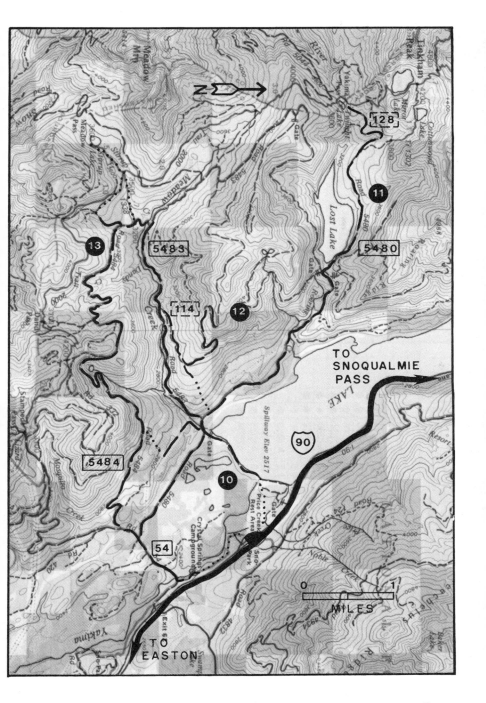

41

Small stream crossed on That Dam Loop

The Tour: From the Sno-Park the trail heads west for 30 feet through the trees then turns abruptly left (south) at an unmarked intersection. Note the narrow road on the right; it is the return leg of the loop. It's also the start of the Another Lost Lake Tour.

Wander through the forest on a trail compacted by snowmobile use. The ups and downs can be fun, but watch out for snowmobiles speeding through. Might has the right-of-way. After a mile in the forest, the trail becomes a road and picnic tables announce Crystal Springs Campground. Shortly beyond is the Stampede Pass road No. 54.

Turn right onto the road, cross the Yakima River, and brace yourself for the recreational equivalent of rush hour on I-5. The road swarms with skiers, snowmobilers, snow cats, and parades of people heading to private cabins. At 1¾ miles ditch the traffic and turn right on Forest Road 5480.

The road is level and fairly straight as it parallels the old railroad grade for the next 1½ miles. At 3¼ miles from the Sno-Park, the loop makes its third right-hand turn. Cross over a snow-covered gate, then ski along the top of the Keechelus Lake Dam. In good weather make this your picnic site, as it's the best viewpoint. Enjoy the snowcapped peaks rising above the lake, and the ice-clogged Yakima River emerging from it.

On the far side of the dam, note the maintenance buildings in a clearing. Descend a ramp off the dam and ski across that clearing on the left side of the buildings. At the far side, head straight into the forest on a narrow cat road paralleling a line of telephone poles leading to an open flood plain and a flagged path across a stream.

Finally, climb the hill along an old, abandoned road heading back to the Sno-Park.

(If the stream is in flood stage, retrace your tracks to the dam maintenance buildings and follow the maintenance road to I-90. It's a ⅛-mile trudge east on the road's dirty snowbank back to the Sno-Park.)

YAKIMA RIVER

11 ANOTHER LOST LAKE

Skill level: intermediate
Round trip: 10 miles
Skiing time: 5 hours
Elevation gain: 800 feet
High point: 3200 feet

Best: mid-December–February
Avalanche potential: moderate
Map: Green Trails, Snoqualmie Pass

Map on page 41

We always wonder why this country has so many "Lost Lakes." Was it a misplaced early explorer, or a modern-day skier who got disoriented in the maze of logging roads crisscrossing these environs? Pay attention to

Keechelus Lake from Lost Lake Road

the landmarks and you'll find this pretty lake in its cradle of high hills without much trouble. Fail to pay attention and you'll join those early explorers, wandering up the wrong valley.

Access: Drive Interstate 90 east 9.1 miles from Snoqualmie Pass to the eastbound Price Creek Sno-Park/Rest Area (2480 feet). (Westbound traffic must continue on to the Hyak–Rocky Run Exit 54 to turn around and return to the Sno-Park. No walking across the highway from the westbound Sno-Park is allowed.)

The Tour: Head into the forest from the Sno-Park on the snowmobile trail for approximately 30 feet. At an unmarked intersection, turn right onto a narrow, somewhat overgrown road heading away from the main flow of traffic. Descend the short, steep hill to a swampy area and cross a small stream, then turn left to negotiate the two channels of a larger stream. (Branches and sticks help form a platform for the snow, but use caution crossing the stream—be prepared to remove skis. If the stream is in flood, go back to the Sno-Park and walk the snowbank west along the edge of I-90 for ⅛ mile to a gated maintenance road and ski to the Keechelus Lake Dam.)

Once across the stream, climb a 10-foot bank to a level bench, turn right, and head north for 1000 feet to a narrow cat road. Turn left and follow the telephone lines to the dam forming Keechelus Lake. Using the ramp on the right side of the dam maintenance buildings, climb up to the road traversing the top of the dam. Here you'll witness fine views of the lake and surrounding peaks. After you put the camera away, head left along the top of the dam for 1 mile to Road 5480.

Ski straight ahead, across the abandoned Milwaukee Railroad bed and Meadow Creek. Pass the junction with Meadow Creek road No. 5483 and continue straight on Road 5480. The road is fairly flat until it reaches a small community of resort homes at Roaring Creek (3½ miles). Now the work begins.

Arrive at a narrow pass at 4½ miles. Cross over to a view of Lost Lake (3089 feet) at the base of a valley, completely clearcut except for a fringe of trees encircling the lake. If staying the night, you'll find nice camping along the northwest side of the lake.

After cheese and rolls, it is time to explore. Continue around the lake for another 1½ miles on Road 5480 then go left on Road (5480)128. Leave this road just above Yakima Pass and ski up a short, steep clearcut to a forested saddle and Mirror Lake (4195 feet) nestled at the base of Tinkham Peak.

If your batteries are still charged, consider a loop trip. Ski toward Yakima Pass and descend 200 feet to little Twilight Lake, then head south to the ridge top and intersect one of several logging spur roads from Meadow Creek Valley. Consult your map for various ways back to the dam and Sno-Park.

YAKIMA RIVER

12 YAKIMA VALLEY OVERVIEW

Skill level: intermediate
Round trip: 10 miles
Skiing time: 5 hours
Elevation gain: 1420 feet
High point: 3900 feet

Best: mid-December–March
Avalanche potential: moderate
Map: Green Trails, Snoqualmie Pass

Map on page 41

You wouldn't want to visit the hills overlooking the Yakima Valley in the summer. The area was so intensely logged it's hard to find a tree to hide behind. Ironically, snows of winter mask the scars of summer— kind of the way some women hide beneath a mask of makeup.

What is visible to the winter traveler, then, is a proliferation of viewpoints and overlooks. From the multitude of viewpoints, one particular area offers an outstanding overview of the Yakima River Valley from the Snoqualmie Pass peaks down the length of Keechelus Lake, east over Amabilis Mountain, and all the way to Easton.

Access: Drive Interstate 90 to the eastbound Price Creek Sno-Park/Rest Area (2480 feet; see Tour 10 for directions).

The Tour: Following the route as described in Tour 11, ski 1½ miles across the Keechelus Lake Dam to Lost Lake road No. 5480. Ski straight ahead, crossing the railroad tracks and the Meadow Creek Bridge, before reaching the Meadow Creek intersection. Here a choice of an approach by

Keechelus Lake Dam and Yakima Valley from the Overview

road or a combination of road and clearcut awaits you. The latter option is best left to skiers with advanced skills.

The road approach follows Meadow Creek road No. 5483, the left fork, climbing uphill into a broad valley. At the 3-mile mark, near the edge of endless clearcuts (2900 feet), turn right on Road (5483)114 and climb steadily through a band of second-growth forest to open clearcuts. At the end of a long switchback at 5 miles, the road arrives at an old logging landing stage, the objective of the climb (3900 feet). The road climbs on, heading west over Meadow Creek Valley, but if you've come for the views it doesn't get any better than this. Might as well sit down and enjoy a beer.

For an Alternate Route to the overview, ski on past the turn to Meadow Creek road No. 5483. Continue about 500 feet farther toward Lost Lake before turning left on the next road (no road numbers posted in 1988). The road climbs steeply (climbing skins very helpful here) through a clearcut to the powerline road. Turn left and follow this road for about ⅛ mile. Now find a thin section in the band of trees above and bushwhack up to the next clearcut. Continue up to Road (5483)114, which you'll intersect about 1 mile below the overview.

Anyone with a passable telemark or a good kick-turn will discover this tour has a lot more to offer than good views. You'll get plenty of thrills following the Alternate Route down through the clearcuts to the Lost Lake road. Be sure to stay on the right of the clearcut slopes during the descent; the left side is steep and prone to sliding.

13 THE DANDY LOOPS

Skill level: intermediate
Round trip: 10½ miles
Skiing time: 6 hours
Elevation gain: 1620 feet
High point: 4100 feet

Best: December–March
Avalanche potential: moderate
Map: Green Trails, Snoqualmie Pass

Map on page 41

This tour has it all: flat country for striding, gliding, and skating; gentle upgrades for an aerobic workout; lunch spots complete with expansive views; and an exhilarating descent (with options for telemarkers). It's not called the Dandy Loops for nothing, you know.

Access: Drive east from Snoqualmie Pass on Interstate 90 to Price Creek Sno-Park/Rest Area (2480 feet; see Tour 10).

The Tour: Ski across the Keechelus Lake Dam (see Tour 11 for directions). At the end of the dam road, continue straight on Road 5480, crossing the railroad grade and Meadow Creek. Turn left on Road 5483 and ski through a thin fringe of trees, then along the bald hillsides of Meadow Creek Valley. At 4½ miles (3160 feet), turn left onto the Dandy Creek road No. 5484, where the aerobic portion of your workout begins. Cross Meadow Creek and then "feel the burn" as you begin the long slog upward.

Pass the trail to Stirrup Lake at 4¾ miles. At 5 miles a spur road cuts off to the right, a tempting sidetrip to a small saddle. At 5¾ miles the road enters one of the rare groves of trees in this area and crosses Dandy Creek (3390 feet). Say hello to a life form that is nearly extinct in this beautifully managed parcel of Forest Service land. Then say goodbye because it's quickly back to the clearcuts.

At 6 miles the road skirts around a rugged basin, at the lowest end of Dandy Pass. A final push brings its reward with a high point at 4100 feet and views over the entire Meadow Creek Valley, Dandy Pass, and a dandy view of Mount Rainier. Peak baggers can conquer the clearcut hill just 100 feet above. The road skirts around the crest of the hill to begin its long descent back to the valley floor. The downward plunge begins with a sweeping semicircle around a small pond. (If the snow is stable, consider a shortcut down and across the frozen pond to the road on the far side.)

Beyond the pond skiers can swoosh across a steep open hillside, past a band of trees, through a steep logging clearing, and then into a second clearing. Here you can make a major shortcut as follows: ski down the clearcut, angling right at the base to reach the lowest point, where a road is found. Continue descending until the powerlines are reached, then head left toward Meadow Creek. The road crosses under the powerlines

Dandy Pass area, Tinkham Peak in distance

several times before a final steep dropoff to the east. With luck, you'll find yourself at the Meadow Creek Bridge. Ski the dam route back to the car. (Using the shortcut makes the round trip 9½ miles long.)

If you don't trust your luck on unsigned roads, continue down Road 5484 to the Stampede Pass road No. 54. Turn left, ski across the railroad tracks, and ½ mile beyond cross the Yakima River. At Crystal Springs Campground go left and follow the snowmobile route upriver to the Sno-Park.

14 STAMPEDE PASS

Stampede Pass

Skill level: intermediate
Round trip: 12 miles
Skiing time: 6 hours
Elevation gain: 1300 feet
High point: 3700 feet
Best: December–April
Avalanche potential: low
Maps: Green Trails,
  Snoqualmie Pass

Loop Trip

Skill level: advanced
Round trip: 12 miles
Skiing time: 7 hours
Elevation gain: 1960 feet
High point: 4360 feet
Best: December–April
Avalanche potential: moderate
Maps: Green Trails,
  Snoqualmie Pass

Miles of undulating roads to climb, high-speed descents through open clearcuts, choice winter campsites, and delightful views all contribute to making Stampede Pass a most enjoyable day or weekend ski tour. All levels and ages of skiers could enjoy this trip but, due to the narrowness of some roads and bonzo snowmobilers rocketing about, at least intermediate-level skills are important if you wish to avoid making a claim on your health-insurance policy.

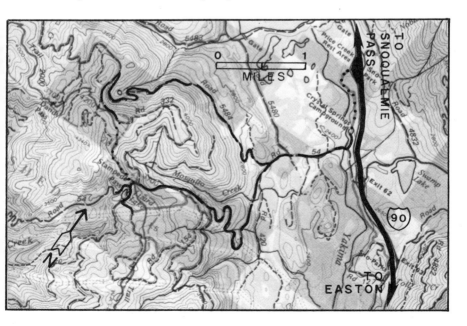

Exploring north of Stampede Pass

Access: Drive Interstate 90 east from Snoqualmie Pass 9.1 miles to the eastbound Price Creek Sno-Park/Rest Area (2400 feet; see Tour 10 for directions).

The Tour: Ski the snowmobile trail from the Sno-Park 1 mile to the Stampede Pass road No. 54 (see Tour 10 for details).

Turn right on the gentle Stampede Pass Road, crossing the Yakima River, and ski across the flat valley floor. At 1¾ miles the road reaches a major intersection in a broad clearing; the right road (No. 5480) goes north around Keechelus Lake while the road to Stampede Pass continues straight across the clearing. After 2 miles, a railroad grade is crossed and the road swings left, starting the long climb to the pass. (in 100 feet pass Road 5484 on the right, the return leg of the loop trip.)

Climb steadily to a powerline clearing at 3½ miles, which marks the beginning of a short series of switchbacks and excellent views of the Yakima River Valley, Amabilis Mountain, and the Keechelus Ridge area. Near the 5-mile mark you'll encounter another major intersection as Road 41 to Easton (popular with snowmobilers) branches left. The Stampede Pass Road now leaves the views and carves across the steep walls of Mosquito Creek Valley to reach the 3700-foot pass at 6 miles, just as Mount Rainier pops into view.

From Stampede Pass you can explore miles of connecting roads and open ridge tops. A favorite destination is Lizard Lake, a small, sheltered pond just 300 feet beyond the pass on the left. Also consider a sidetrip to the U.S. government weather station located 1½ miles south (reached by a small road leaving from Lizard Lake). Excellent campsites abound throughout this area.

For the advanced skier reaching for a Franz Klammer rush, the return trip can be made as a loop. From Stampede Pass follow the narrow bench above the north side of the road left for about 500 feet, then contour up to the base of a steep slope. Climb the slope on the left side where timber helps stabilize the snow. Once on the ridge top the ski route follows the path of the Pacific Crest Trail north. Using the ridge as a guide, ski just to the west of the crest and follow it over a second hill to a large clearcut valley. Continue following the ridge as it meanders in a northwesterly direction to its end on a hilltop (4360 feet) overlooking clearcut Meadow Creek Valley. Turn left and ski the ridge down to a logging road in the small saddle.

Ski the logging road across the saddle to the base of a small hill. Here a choice of routes must be made. If the prevailing winds have been blowing from the south, ski around the right side of the hill, staying on the road. If winds have been blowing from the north, causing snow to accumulate on the south side, ski over the top of the small hill to avoid a potential slab avalanche. If in doubt, ski over the top.

Once around or over the final hill, turn left (east) and head down on Road 5484 for 3 miles back to the Stampede Pass Road, reaching the old railroad grade at 10 miles. A final 2 miles of skiing on level ground returns you to the Sno-Park.

Skier on the Pacific Crest Trail, north of Stampede Pass

51

15 KACHESS LAKE CAMPGROUND

Skill level: basic
Round trip: 4 miles to campground
Skiing time: 2 hours
Elevation loss: 20 feet
High point: 2320 feet

Best: January–February
Avalanche potential: none
Maps: Green Trails, Snoqualmie
  Pass and Kachess Lake

The tour to Kachess Lake Campground is especially good for beginners, groups with varying abilities, or first-time winter campers. A gentle road swings around the lakeshore to forests of tall trees and a

Box Canyon Creek

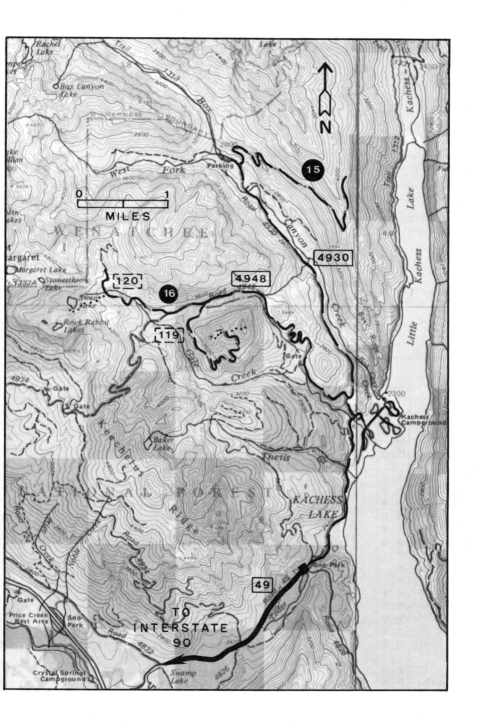

Rachel Lake

Box Canyon Lake

Lake Lillian

Twin Lakes

Mt Margaret

Margaret Lake

Stonesthrow Lake

Swan Lake

Rock Rabbit Lakes

Trail 1313

Box Canyon

West Fork

Parking

WILDERNESS BOUNDARY

WENATCHEE

15

N

0   1
MILES

Road

Canyon

Creek

Box Ridge

Trail 1322

Kachess

Kachess Lake

Little Kachess

4930

120

16

4948

4948

119

Road

Gate Creek

Gate

Baker Lake

Thetis

Kachess Campground

2300

NATIONAL FOREST

KACHESS LAKE

Kachelus Ridge

Road

Road

Noble Creek

Gate

Price Creek Rest Area

Sno-Park

Sno-Park

49

Road 4818

TO INTERSTATE 90

Road 4832

Crystal Springs Campground

Swamp Lake

4826

Road 4826

53

Snow and fog-bound Kachess Lake

pleasant campground. Several miles of skiing in the campground and miles of road beyond it also tempt stronger skiers to work up a sweat.

Access: Follow Interstate 90 for 10.2 miles east of Snoqualmie Pass to Exit 62, Stampede Pass–Kachess Lake. Drive east toward Kachess Lake for 3.3 miles to the long Sno-Park. Parking is only allowed on the south side of the road (2320 feet). On busy weekends the area fills up fast, so try to arrive before 9 A.M.

The Tour: The few snowmobiles that use this area compact the entire road, removing all ski tracks and creating a set of roller-coaster bumps. If the Forest Service enacted a policy confining machines to one side of the road, skiers could speed along in more comfortable sets of tracks on their side of the road. If you are interested in promoting the "skier side of the road" concept, write the Cle Elum Ranger District, P.O. Box 51, Cle Elum, Washington 98922.

From the parking area a gentle descent leads to a broad view up and down Kachess Lake reservoir and across the partially shaved Kachess Ridge. After a brief opening, the road heads away from the lake and back into forest.

After 1½ miles, cross Gale Creek, which marks the entrance to Kachess Lake Campground. Several hours can be spent investigating this sprawling area. The campground loops make excellent racetracks, while nature loops offer challenging courses around the trees.

Skiers who would like to log a few more miles can stride along Forest Road 4930 for another 4 miles to the Rachel Lake trailhead. No sweeping panoramas await as you tour along Box Canyon Creek, but the steep-walled valley is very beautiful. Snow-plastered hillsides, towering evergreens with white coats, and ice sculptures along the banks of the creek all await you. Elevation gain for these extra miles is only 330 feet.

16 SWAN LAKE

Skill level: advanced basic
Round trip: 10 miles
Skiing time: 6 hours
Elevation gain: 1450 feet
High point: 4050 feet

Best: April–May
Avalanche potential: low
Map: Green Trails, Snoqualmie Pass

Map on page 53

Like most roads in the area, the Swan Lake environs are a snowmobile playground. For peace, quiet, and safety, ski here in April and May when the macho men have "summerized" their $4000 toys. This coincides with the return of the songbirds to the higher elevations, warmer days, longer hours of sunshine, brighter burns, and off-color jokes concerning the fate of those who fall down while wearing shorts.

In the spring you'll find this an enjoyable tour. You'll follow forested roads to the open slopes of Gale Creek Valley, and ultimately climb to a small lake nestled in a glade of trees below the east face of Mount Margaret. If views rather than serenity are the objective, an alternate route leads to the top of a 3800-foot hill overlooking the valley, Kachess Lake, and the rocky summits of Kachess Ridge.

Swan Lake and Mount Margaret

Access: Drive 10.2 miles east of Snoqualmie Pass on I-90 to Exit 62. Follow Forest Road 49 to Kachess Lake Campground (6 miles). Turn left on Road 4930, go .6 mile, then turn left again on Road No. 4948 and follow it to the snow. The mileages for this tour are figured from the junction of Roads 4930 and 4948.

The Tour: The first mile through clearcuts climbs quite steeply. Enjoy the views over Kachess Lake Reservoir. In 1¼ miles the road starts switchbacking, passing through a narrow V-shaped valley, and then levels off in the broad Gale Creek Valley, 2¾ miles from the junction. At 3¼ miles reach a junction with Road (4948)119, the alternate tour destination to a panoramic viewpoint. At 3½ miles turn right on Road (4948)120, climbing steadily. The road crosses Gale Creek for the first time at 4¼ miles and recrosses the creek at 4½ miles.

Leave the road 300 feet before the second crossing and turn uphill on a rough spur road (No. 124). Ski this spur while it heads up and to the right. When it turns left, branch off into the forest. In the summer a broad trail leads to the lake. In the winter the trail disappears and the creek serves as an excellent guide. Keeping the creek on the right, you reach the lake (4050 feet) after ½ mile. Enjoy sunbathing, picnicking, and views of Mount Margaret from the edge of the lake, avoiding the rather soggy center section.

Reach the alternate destination, on Road (4948)119, by spiraling up the 3800-foot clearcut hill on the east side of Gale Creek Valley. Either follow the road 2 miles to the top or, if enough snow exists, switchback up the open slopes. There is little avalanche hazard on the road, but a heavy snow pack may make the clearcut slopes hazardous. The road ends in the saddle between two hilltops. Take your pick of the east and west summits for the best view, then take advantage of the spring conditions—dig yourself a private tanning booth and relax.

Bear tracks in the spring snow

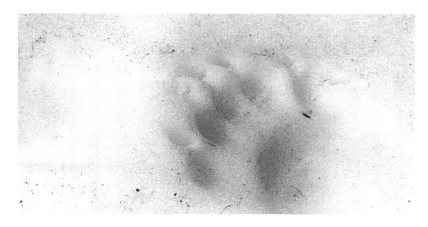

Keechelus Lake from Amabilis Mountain

17 AMABILIS MOUNTAIN

Skill level: intermediate
Round trip: 9 miles
Skiing time: 5 hours
Elevation gain: 2154 feet

High point: 4554 feet
Best: January–March
Avalanche potential: low
Map: Green Trails, Snoqualmie Pass

Ski to the summit of 4554-foot Amabilis Mountain on a wide, well-graded logging road. Near the top set out on a tour of more than 1½ miles along a gleaming ridge with open views of Kachess and Keechelus lakes, Stampede Pass, Mount Catherine, Silver Peak, and above all Mount Rainier. Make a looping return on a different logging road, or head straight down the open clearcuts for a breathtaking telemark descent.

Access: Drive Interstate 90 east from Snoqualmie Pass 10.3 miles and go off on Cabin Creek Exit 63 to the Sno-Parks on the west side of the freeway (2189 feet). Arrive early; latecomers may find the two lots full.

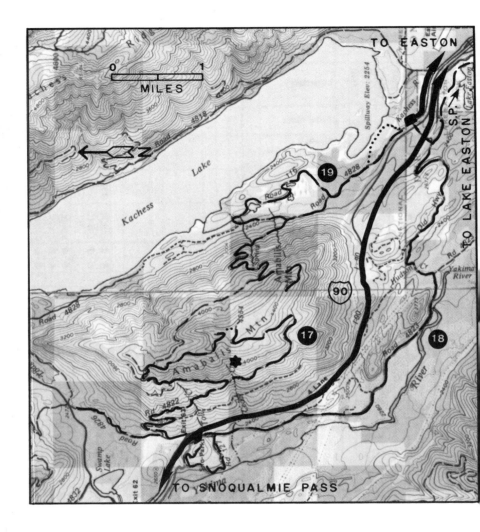

The Tour: Cross to the north side of the freeway on the overpass to Kachess Lake Road. Ski past Trollhaugen Hut, a cross-country racing club, and please stay off the carefully groomed tracks. Beyond the hut the road rounds a corner and splits. Go right on Amabilis Mountain Road and immediately start to climb. The way switchbacks uphill, passing several old spurs, first to the left, then to the right. Occasional windows in the forest give glimpses of massive Keechelus Ridge and the Swamp Lake area.

The first major intersection is at 2 miles (3300 feet). This is the start of the loop and either direction will reach the top; for best enjoyment of the scenery go left. The next mile traverses into a clearcut at the north end of the mountain, switchbacks just below the ridge top, and ascends open slopes. From here on the road often is windswept and hard to follow. When visibility is poor, make the ridge top your turnaround. The final mile lies along the crest and leads, first in open clearcut then back in the trees on a logging road, to the site of an old radio tower. If the road is obscure, simply stay on the west side of the ridge to gain the summit.

For the loop return, in stable conditions only, take the road west from the beacon site, follow the forest road back to close the loop at 6 miles. This leg of the loop crosses a steep avalanche chute and should not be skied except in times of low avalanche hazard.

YAKIMA RIVER

18 CABIN CREEK

Cabin Creek Loop
Skill level: basic
Round trip: 1 mile
Skiing time: 1 hour
Elevation gain: 100 feet
High point: 2560 feet
Best: January–February
Avalanche potential: none
Map: Green Trails, Snoqualmie Pass

Map on page 58

Lake Easton Trail
Skill level: advanced basic
One way: 9½ miles
Skiing time: 3 hours
Elevation loss: 200 feet
High point: 2450 feet
Best: January–February
Avalanche potential: none
Maps: Green Trails, Snoqualmie Pass and Kachess Lake

In the midst of mountain country where all the scenery is vertical, the Cabin Creek area features valley flats and rolling hills, open and gentle terrain ideal for beginners to perfect their balance and racers to achieve speed. Two trips can be made. The first is a short, scenic loop trip that starts and ends at the parking lot. The second follows an old road to Lake Easton State Park.

Access: Drive Interstate 90 east from Snoqualmie Pass 10.3 miles to Cabin Creek Exit 63. Park in the large Sno-Park on the south side (2450 feet).

Cabin Creek Loop: The loop trip starts from the lower end of the Sno-Park and returns to the upper end. Follow the sign toward a viewpoint, leaving the parking lot on the right (west) side. Descend gently through second growth to open meadows. Stay right at the first intersection. (Skiers may also enjoy a sidetrip cruise out in the meadows.) At all intersections keep the small knoll on your right side. In ½ mile the Yakima

Cabin Creek Loop

River meanders by the trail, then disappears in forest. In ¼ mile more a large clearcut is crossed. Ski to the top for views east to Amabilis Mountain (Tour 17), and southwest to Stampede Pass.

To close the loop, ski out through the lower southeast corner of the clearcut to the Sno-Park entrance.

Lake Easton Trail: The Lake Easton Trail is 9½ miles one way, following the old, old, old Snoqualmie Pass Road from Cabin Creek to Lake Easton State Park. The trip requires endurance but is suitable for all levels of skiers.

YAKIMA RIVER

19 SOUTH KACHESS LAKE

Marsh Loops

Skill level: basic
Round trip: 6 miles
Skiing time: 3 hours
Elevation gain: 80 feet
High point: 2400 feet
Best: January–February
Avalanche potential: none
Map: Green Trails, Kachess Lake

Map on page 58

Lake Easton

Skill level: advanced basic
Round trip: 6 miles
Skiing time: 3 hours
Elevation gain: 300 feet
High point: 2500 feet
Best: January–February
Avalanche potential: none
Maps: Green Trails, Easton and
*   Kachess Lake*

In our opinion the open country at the south end of Kachess Lake is the best terrain for beginning skiers in the entire Snoqualmie Pass area. The skiing is safe and easy in all weather conditions and the rolling hills found here are fun for first-timers.

Two trips are suggested below. The Marsh Loop Ski Trails, marked by the Forest Service, guide the skier along the scenic Kachess Lake shore and around snow-blanketed marshes at the base of Amabilis Mountain. The Lake Easton Trail borders the lake, then follows the Old Snoqualmie Pass Highway to a viewpoint overlooking the Yakima River Valley.

Access: Drive Interstate 90 east 16.8 miles from Snoqualmie Pass to Exit 70.

Marsh Loops: From Exit 70, turn left on Sparks Road and drive 1.2 miles to the Sno-Park at road's end (2320 feet).

Ski the well-marked Forest Service road, shared by snow machines and skiers, following the trail of blue diamonds on the trees. After ¼ mile go straight through a junction. The road runs through deep woods and is crossed by several streams. In late spring these small streams may melt gaping pits in the snow, inconveniences that help reduce the machine traffic.

After 1¼ miles the dense forest is left behind and another intersection is reached. Here begins the first of the two loops. Bear right and meander around the marshes and ponds, under their blanket of winter white, with views west to snowbound Amabilis Mountain. At 2¾ miles from the Sno-Park is the top of the loop, where the marshes end. Bear left (west) to rejoin the main road and close the first loop at 3½ miles.

Reenter the forest, following your own tracks back ½ mile to the trail junction. Go left (east) on a short, rolling trail to the shore of Kachess Lake and follow an old road paralleling the shore for ½ mile. Near the dam an opening in the trees gives access to the shore, a perfect place to pull out a sandwich and enjoy winter.

From the lake a forest trail heads southwest to rejoin the machine-skier road, closing the second section of the loop. Ski the road for a final ¼ mile back to the start.

Lake Easton: From Exit 70, following the signs to Lake Easton State Park, drive .6 mile along the west side of Interstate 90. Enter the park and

Marsh Loops near Kachess Lake

Marsh Loops Ski Trail

take a right at the ranger's residence. Drive to the end of the road on the shores of Lake Easton (2200 feet).

From the upper right-hand side of the parking area, ski around a gate and follow the Old Snoqualmie Pass Highway around Lake Easton for ¾ mile. Just before the road temporarily ends, jog left on a forest road and ski around the gate marking the end of State Park land. (Note: The snowmobile-skier trail that jogs right near the end of the lake borders the freeway and is totally lacking in esthetics.)

Beyond the State Park ski through a large clearcut to an intersection. To the right a road crosses under Interstate 90 to Sparks Road and the Marsh Loops Sno-Park. Ski straight ahead on the Old Highway, making a leisurely switchback to a second intersection at 2 miles. Go right, winding through a clearcut for 1000 feet, then duck back into the forest for a mile of nearly level skiing.

At 3 miles the Old Highway ends at the edge of a massive clearing. This is a good place to check out the view west toward Cabin Mountain and Stampede Pass before returning to Lake Easton.

20 MORE CABIN CREEK

Skill level: basic
Round trip: 6 miles
Skiing time: 2 hours or more
Elevation loss: 200 feet in first 3 miles

High point: 2800 feet
Best: March–mid-May
Avalanche potential: low
Maps: Green Trails, Easton and Lester

Here's another one of those springtime trips that come into season once the noisy herd of snowmobiles has been put out to pasture. The Cle Elum Ranger District now ranks as Washington's number-one area for snowmobile use, so wintertime skiing may remind you of running with the bulls in Pamplona. However, when the sun gets warm in the lowlands and the dandelions start sprouting in your garden, let the snowmobilers stay home to weed while you go skiing.

Diverse skiing opportunities await you here. Those who have yet to try out their Christmas skis (shame on you) can cruise the wide rolling roads; long-distance skiers will find ample miles to exhaust themselves; and telemarkers will encounter steep, open clearcuts to carve.

Access: Drive Interstate 90 for 17 miles east of Snoqualmie Pass and take Exit 71 at Easton. Drive into town, cross the main street (old Highway 10), then head straight up Cabin Creek Road for .2 mile. After crossing the railroad tracks swing right, remaining on Cabin Creek Road. Drive to the snowline, usually about 1½ miles from town in late March (2800 feet).

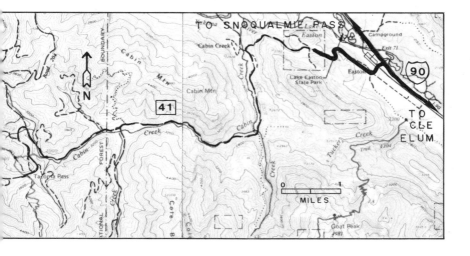

Log-reloading area on the Cabin Creek road

The Tour: The road is groomed for snowmobiles throughout the winter, so expect a solid (i.e., icy) surface in the early morning. Ski along rolling terrain, past a swamp, and through tall timber for nearly 1½ miles before descending to the first viewpoint over the Yakima River and the clearcut slopes of Amabilis Mountain. The road continues dropping to an intersection at 2½ miles. Here, take the left fork (Forest Road 41) and ski to the large log reloading area, a broad open meadow in the winter and a good place for first-time skiers to snack before heading back.

Skiers out for a workout or weekend can continue on up Road 41, which joins a network of roads leading around Cabin Mountain. It's 7 more miles to Tacoma Pass (3400 feet), 15 miles to Stampede Pass, and 30 miles to Snoqualmie Pass. If endless miles of roads fail to motivate you, will a good viewpoint get you off your seat? If so, ski 3 more miles up Cabin Creek to a viewpoint overlooking the entire Keechelus Lake area.

21 JOHN WAYNE TRAIL

Skill level: basic
Round trip: up to 15 miles
Skiing time: up to 7 hours
Elevation loss: 120 feet
High point: 1840 feet

Best: January
Avalanche potential: low
Maps: Green Trails, Cle Elum and
Thorp

A ski tour across the state of Washington—now there's a thought to inspire the fantasy of skiers. Surprisingly, in the future such a dream could materialize along the old Milwaukee Road railroad grade.

When the Milwaukee Road was abandoned by the railroad, the section from Easton to the Idaho border was obtained for the state. It was named John Wayne Pioneer Trail by the hard-working group of equestrians who had the foresight to lobby the legislature before the land was taken over by private interests. The trail is dedicated to all nonmotorized travel—skis and snowshoes in the winter and horses, hikers and mountain bikes in the summer. The state is involved in working out the right of way along the old grade and so far has managed to place 25 miles under State Park jurisdiction. The remainder of the trail is currently under the control of the Department of Natural Resources (DNR) and open to public travel April 15 to May 31 and in October, not very handy for skiers. The DNR currently does not have the resources to maintain the rest of the trail, which is being taken over by adjoining property owners.

The trail starts in the town of Easton and heads through the rural Yakima River Valley, crossing the river twice on airy railroad bridges. The most isolated and scenic section of the trail is the last seven miles, which end at an old tunnel in a narrow, rock-walled gorge of the Yakima River.

Access: Drive 22 miles east of Snoqualmie Pass on Interstate 90 to Exit 84 and drive .7 mile toward Cle Elum. As the road descends into town, turn right, following signs to S. Cle Elum. In the next .3 mile the road passes under the freeway, crosses the Yakima River, enters South Cle Elum, and becomes Fourth Street. Bear left, uphill, .6 mile to an intersection and take a left on Lower Peoh Point Road. Drive 2.2 miles and pass under I-90 again. After driving .6 mile beyond the underpass, park on the wide shoulder along the left side of the road (1840 feet).

The Tour: Ski down the steep embankment to the old railroad, then head east past a small barn and adjacent cows. On the left are the Yakima River and occasional glimpses of the Stuart Range. In 1 mile you'll see the ice-clad Teanaway and Yakima rivers converging.

The trail tunnels through a grove of trees, then returns to the river,

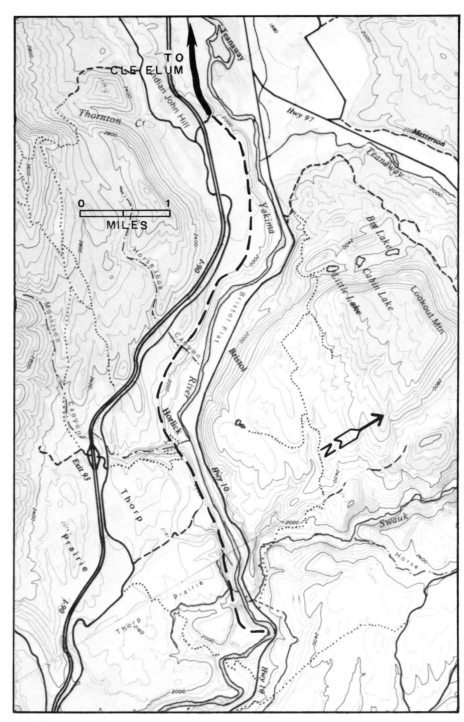

John Wayne Trail at the edge of the Yakima River

passing a broad swath of buzzing powerlines at 2½ miles. Ahead the valley opens into Bristol Flat, an isolated section of level farmland boxed in by hills.

Continue straight ahead on flat terrain, passing a large overflow from an irrigation canal on the hill above. At 4½ miles pass a couple of old shacks, remains of the old town of Horlick. The river now bends to the east as the valley narrows, and on the opposite side Highway 10 climbs above the level of the trail for the first time. The scenery becomes dramatic as the trail cuts through the steep canyon walls only a few feet above the sweeping torrent of the Yakima River.

The trail ends at 7½ miles in a shaded bend of the river where the winter sun rarely penetrates. Here railroad workers built a tunnel rather than blast a bench along the sheer canyon walls of basalt. Turn around here—the section beyond requires a permit. Enjoy the scenery, but do so on day trips only—no camping is allowed on the Duke's trail.

22 WENATCHEE MOUNTAINS

Skill level: *advanced basic*
Round trip: *2 miles or more*
Skiing time: *3 hours–all day*
Elevation gain: *2500 feet*
High point: *5700 feet*
Best: *mid-December–March*
Avalanche potential: *low*
Map: *Green Trails, Thorp*

Ski trail markers

If you are a gambler at heart, the ski terrain at the southwest end of the Wenatchee Mountains will captivate you. "What's the big gamble?" you ask. "Snow," we reply. Some days you'll encounter massive amounts of unconsolidated snow blanketing the slopes. A few days later, entire hillsides are once again naked.

Hit the snow right and you'll experience lovely skiing over open hillsides and rolling ridge tops with panoramic views. You'll also find miles of roads and trails to explore, allowing for excellent day and overnight trips. Hit it wrong and you'll be confined to the roads, or witness rocks carving glacial valleys into the bases of your skis. Obviously, if you are not a gambler, a few phone calls can help you decide whether to make the pilgrimage to this unpredictable neck of the woods.

Access: Drive Interstate 90 to Ellensburg and take Exit 106, then turn north. Immediately off the overpass is a four-way intersection with gas stations, fast-food joints, and few road signs. Turn left (west) on an unmarked road and drive 1.3 miles to another four-way intersection. Go left on Highway 10, following it north 1.2 miles before turning right on to Highway 97. Follow the highway for 1 mile, then turn right on Lower Green Canyon Road and drive north 5 miles to its end. Turn left and drive on Reecer Creek Road 2.8 miles to the Sno-Park located at the end of the county road.

The Sno-Park here is somewhat peculiar. It starts at the end of the county road (2700 feet), but the road is normally plowed for another 2 miles to a small parking area at 3200 feet. Where you park will vary with the weather and the day.

The Tour: The snowmobiles have developed a shortcut trail from the parking area straight up the hill to meet the road above. The lower section of this trail is extremely steep and best avoided. Ski the road up the first looping switchback to the top of a bench, where it is possible to leave the road and ski up the open hill using the ridge line as a guide. The road

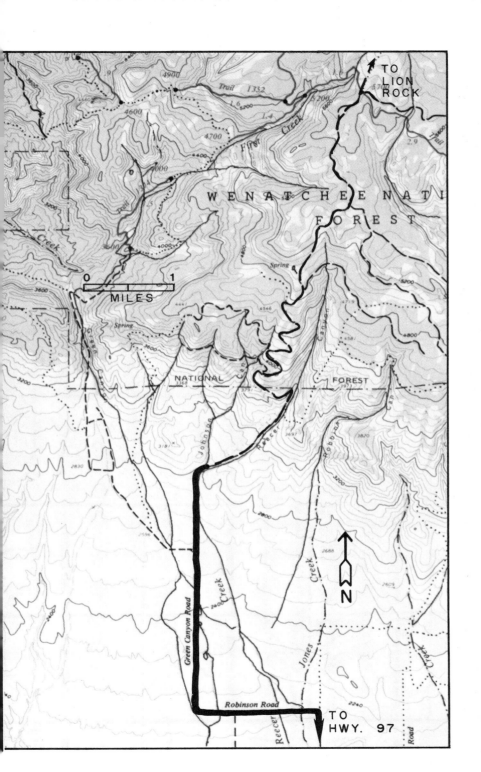

TO LION ROCK

Trail 1352

1.0

1.4

First Creek

2.9

WENATCHEE NATI

FOREST

Spring

0   1

MILES

Spring

NATIONAL   FOREST

Johnson

Reecer

Canyon

Green Canyon Road

Creek

Creek

Jones

Creek

Robinson

Creek

N

Robinson Road

Reecer

Road

TO HWY. 97

Yakima River Valley viewed from Reecer Creek Road

continues to switchback, and skiers climbing the ridge can expect to cross it several times.

Views out over Ellensburg's vast plains, the Cascades, Mount Adams and Mount Rainier are outstanding. The pine forests of the east side are also outstanding. Trees are small and thinly spread, allowing for cross-country skiing in the true sense of the word—a refreshing change for west-siders. Reecer Canyon, falling away on the right, is a gash in the open hillside, with striking cliffs of columnar basalt.

At 4 miles (4800 feet) the switchbacks end at a group of summer homes. Return to the road here as it continues to climb, reaching a broad intersection at 5 miles (5700 feet). You have now reached the southern end of Table Mountain. You'll find excellent touring here and limitless campsites in all directions—help yourself.

If time permits, ski north 6 miles to Lion Rock and an outstanding view over the Yakima River Valley and Taneum Ridge area. If time is limited check out the "Skier Only" trails. Start from the intersection and go straight following the blue diamonds; the first is located right above the road sign. Ski into the trees following the blue diamonds to a clearing, where the Ellensburg Cross-Country Ski Club has a small warming hut. Several other trails start from the hut.

23 HEX MOUNTAIN

Skill level: advanced
Round trip: 8 miles
Skiing time: 6 hours
Elevation gain: 2647 feet

High point: 5034 feet
Best: December–April
Avalanche potential: low
Map: Green Trails, Kachess Lake

You might call Hex Mountain an "exceptional" backcountry tour. Routefinding is exceptionally confusing on the logging-road portion of the tour but exceptionally easy on the backcountry portion. The tour is exceptionally free from avalanche hazard, making it skiable in all conditions. The descent through open forest and meadows provides exceptional fun. Finally, you'll find some exceptional views from the summit of this mountain.

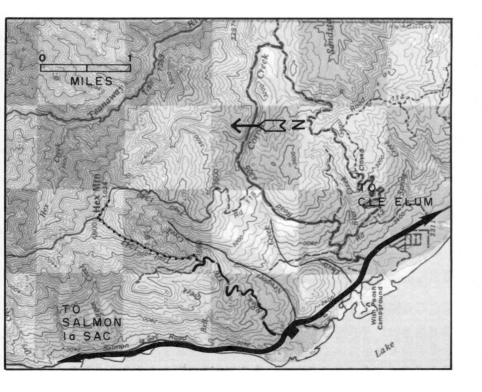

Ridge leading to summit of Hex Mountain

There are two approaches to Hex Mountain. The approach described here is the shorter and steeper of the two. The longer approach (from Road 4305 and Trail 1340) is exceptionally overrun by snowmobiles on weekends. (Rumor says it is a good midweek tour.)

Access: Drive Interstate 90 to Exit 80, Salmon la Sac and Roslyn. Go east to State Route 903, then take a left and drive north 8.7 miles, passing through Roslyn, Ronald, and Lakedale. Park in a small turnout on the left side of the road at Newport Creek (2387 feet).

The Tour: From the turnout, walk north on the road for .1 mile to Forest Road (4300)116 (the first road on the right). Don the skis here and start the climb. In 1988 the forest around Road (4300)116 was being selectively cut, and roads and skid roads were sprouting everywhere. As a result, our explanation may seem inaccurate and routefinding will be a challenge for the first 1½ miles of the tour.

As of 1988, the road climbs steeply for the first ⅛ mile, then levels out to contour around a small catch basin. Ignore all side roads as you skirt around the left side of the basin. The road drops, climbs briefly, levels out for a second time, then divides. Take the left fork, traversing uphill. (If the road starts descending steadily, you took the wrong fork.)

Your goal is the summit of the ridge to your left. To reach the ridge the road climbs across the hillside, dips left into a small side valley, then climbs again. Around 3200 feet, the road divides again; stay left.

At 2 miles (3500 feet), the road reaches the ridge top. Leave the road here and ski to the right, heading up the crest of the ridge. Under the snow is Trail 1343 and you may see signs of it, such as blazes on trees and clear passages through the forest.

The ridge climbs (with occasional dips) for 1¾ miles. Stay away from the edges, which are often corniced. At 4900 feet, the ridge you have followed ends on the summit ridge. Go right (southeast) for ¼ mile, first descending, then climbing out of the trees to the open summit of Hex Mountain (5034 feet).

Atop you'll find a lot of scenery to soak in while eating lunch. To the west lie Cle Elum Lake and a host of minor summits between Mount Baldy and Thorp Mountain. To the north rise the rugged summits of Cone Mountain and Davis Peak as well as the rounded slopes of Sasse Mountain. Finally, Table Mountain and the open plains of the Yakima River Valley occupy the eastern view.

Cle Elum Lake from Hex Mountain

24 FRENCH CABIN CREEK

Skill level: intermediate
Round trip: 4–14 miles
Skiing time: 4 hours–2 days
Elevation gain: 1336 feet
High point: 3600 feet

Best: March–mid-May
Avalanche potential: low to moderate
Map: Green Trails, Kachess Lake

A logging road with a number of short spurs leads to a variety of destinations and views, suitable for a good half-day workout, an all-day exploration, or an overnight up the Thorp Creek Trail. The trip is very

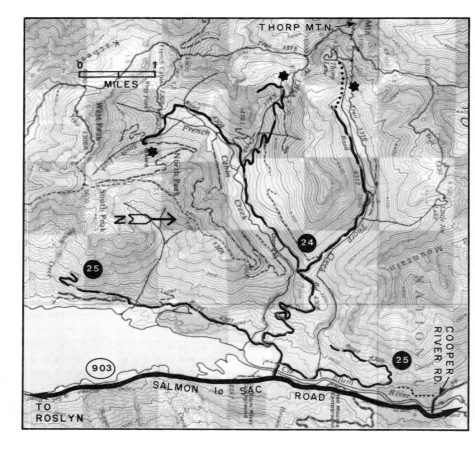

good all winter—assuming the county road can be driven to Salmon la Sac. (In midwinter it is wise to call the Cle Elum Ranger Station to check on this.) Thanks to the Forest Service, however, the French Cabin Creek Road is heavily used on weekends by speeding snowmobiles, and therefore it is best for skiers to come midweek or wait until late spring when the snowmobiles give up.

Access: Go off Interstate 90 on Exit 80 and drive Highway 903, following signs to Salmon la Sac, passing through both Roslyn and Ronald and

Skiing the French Cabin Creek valley below Red Mountain

around Cle Elum Lake. At 12 miles from Roslyn City Hall find the French Cabin Creek Road (2262 feet).

The Tour: The road crosses the Cle Elum River on a concrete bridge and in ¼ mile starts climbing. In the next 2 miles the road gains 1000 feet in a series of five long switchbacks, steep enough for most skiers. To escape snowmobile ruts, the first four switchbacks can be shortcut. As the road climbs, the face of Red Mountain comes in view, seemingly towering overhead, a spectacular sight after a fresh snowfall. At 2½ miles the road levels and enters French Cabin Creek Valley.

Thorp Creek Trail: Energetic skiers can do an overnight ski tour to Thorp Lake, capped by an ascent (if conditions warrant) of 5854-foot Thorp Mountain. (Mountaineer nordic skiers can handle the peak, but most skiers are better off on alpine skis.) At 3½ miles on the main road go off right on Thorp Creek Road about 1 mile to its end. Continue up the valley 3 more miles to the lake. The forest travel is not easy—but does stop the machines. If the opportunity presents itself, cross to the north side of the creek, where the going is somewhat better.

Camp at the lake in forest well away from any possible avalanche (but not under a tree topped with a mushroom of snow). Do not attempt the open slopes to the ridge unless the snow is stable.

North Peak Road: At 4 miles go left on a logging road that climbs to clearcuts on North Peak; views are great of Red Mountain and up the Salmon la Sac Valley.

Knox Creek: At 5 miles go right on Knox Creek Road and climb 2 miles to the end at the foot of a large, steep mountain meadow. (Avalanche hazard is possible in the meadow.)

French Cabin Mountain: Follow the main road to its end at 7 miles in clearcuts and mountain meadows under French Cabin Mountain.

25 CLE ELUM RIVER

Skill level: basic
Round trip: 2–5 miles
Skiing time: 1–2 hours
Elevation gain: none
High point: 2400 feet

Best: January–March
Avalanche potential: none
Map: Green Trails, Kachess Lake

Map on page 74

A delightful valley-bottom tour within constant sight and sound of the Cle Elum River, with a fair chance of getting away from sight and sound of snowmobiles.

The trip can either start from French Cabin Creek Road (Tour 24) or Cooper River Road (Tour 28). Unfortunately, steep cliffs and the crossing of Thorp Creek make it impossible to start at one point and finish at the other.

Davis Peak from the Cle Elum River

French Cabin Creek: From French Cabin Creek Road cross the Cle Elum River bridge and in ¼ mile find a spur road to the right. Follow it 2 miles to the start of the uphill—or continue 1½ miles into clearcuts and views. If there are snowmobiles, stay off the spur road and instead follow as closely as possible along the river. If snowmobiles are buzzing around and ruining your ski tracks, weave between the trees.

Cooper River Road: From Cooper River Road cross the Cle Elum River on a concrete bridge and as soon as practical leave the road on the downstream side and follow as close to the river as you can. In roughly 1 mile cliffs and creeks stop progress.

CLE ELUM LAKE

26 JOLLY AND JOLLY TOO

Jolly Road
Skill level: basic
Round trip: 8 miles
Skiing time: 3 hours
Elevation gain: 1720 feet
High point: 4000 feet
Best: January–mid-April
Avalanche potential: low
Map: Green Trails, Kachess Lake

Jolly Too Road
Skill level: advanced basic
Round trip: 11 miles
Skiing time: 4 hours
Elevation gain: up to 3040 feet
High point: 5400 feet
Best: January–mid-April
Avalanche potential: low
Map: Green Trails, Kachess Lake

Map on page 81

Two fun logging roads on the east side of the Cle Elum River climb to open slopes and grand overlooks of the Cle Elum River Valley to French Cabin Creek, Red Mountain, and the Dutch Miller Gap peaks. From Jolly Too other views extend north to Davis Peak and Mount Daniel. Because they are too short to interest snowmobilers, the roads generally are left to quieter winter travelers, although there is no official designation to ensure this.

Access: Go off Interstate 90 on Exit 80 and drive Highway 903 through the towns of Roslyn and Ronald and past Cle Elum Lake. At 13.6 miles from Roslyn City Hall park in a very small, plowed turnout on the right side of the road. There are no signs, but this is the start of Jolly Road (2300 feet).

The Tour: In 1 mile of gentle climbing the road gains a large bench (2500 feet). The several-acre expanse of low, rolling bumps and flat bowls is ideal for family play. For views continue up the road another mile to the base of a large clearcut. In stable snow conditions ascend approximately 700 feet to the top of the clearcut, for the sheer joy of carving a set of turns or sitzmarks on the way back down.

A Jolly Road

Jolly Too Road starts 15.2 miles from Roslyn City Hall. Park only in the small, plowed area on the right side of the road. If there is no parking space available, return .4 mile to Cooper River Road and walk back.

Jolly Too Road is very similar to Jolly Road except a little steeper. Be sure and ski at least 2½ miles to a superb viewpoint north and west. At 4 miles the road divides. The right fork heads out into the clearcuts and ends. The left fork continues on for 1½ more miles over the top of Sasse Ridge to end at 5400 feet on a ridge top overlooking the North Fork Teanaway River Basin and Jolly Mountain to the southeast. This is the edge of the backcountry and some mountaineering skills are required to continue on (see Tour 27).

Skier nearing the summit of Jolly Mountain

CLE ELUM LAKE

27 JOLLY MOUNTAIN

Skill level: advanced
Round trip: 15 miles
Skiing time: 8 hours
Elevation gain: 4163 feet

High point: 6443 feet
Best: December–April
Avalanche potential: moderate
Map: Green Trails, Kachess Lake

Jolly Mountain provides an excellent introduction to mountain skiing with its enjoyable summit and impressive views. Easy navigation, lack of hazards (except near the summit), few technical difficulties, and premier picnic spots also combine to make this tour a popular one.

Access: Take Exit 80 off Interstate 90 and drive Highway 903 through the towns of Roslyn and Ronald and on past Cle Elum Lake. At 15.2 miles from Roslyn City Hall (or .4 mile past the Cooper River Road), watch for Forest Road 4315 on the right. Park off the road in the small two-car space (2280 feet).

The Tour: For the next 4½ miles, ski up the logging road past open clearcuts. Better yet, put on climbing skins and make a beeline toward the top of the ridge where the road divides. Take the left fork and follow it past one long switchback to the summit of Sasse Ridge (4980 feet).

Now follow the road east along the ridge top, overlooking the broad basin of the West Fork Teanaway River. When the road ends after 5½ miles (5400 feet), continue along the crest of the ridge following the snow-covered Sasse Ridge Trail.

Jolly Mountain comes into view across the valley, as do the profiles of Davis Peak, Cone Mountain, and Red Mountain. After 6½ miles, the ridge rounds the end of a basin and reaches a 6100-foot high point. Follow the ridge south, descending across a saddle to Jolly Mountain.

For the final ascent, follow the north ridge, staying as close to the crest as possible. Steep slopes here create some avalanche hazard in unstable conditions. The summit (6443 feet) is reached at 7½ miles. Make a cautious 360-degree turn on the narrow rib looking south to Mount Rainier, down to Cle Elum Lake, west to the Dutch Miller Gap peaks, north to Mount Daniel, and east to Mount Stuart. West and just below the summit is a broad open bench perfectly situated for MTRs (maximum tanning rays) and a picnic. Time for some heavy-duty TM (tan maintenance).

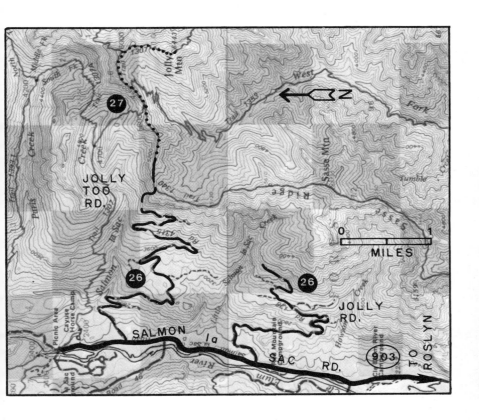

28 PETE LAKE AND COOPER PASS

Skill level: advanced basic
Round trip: 5–22 miles
Skiing time: 3 hours–overnight
Elevation gain: 1000 feet
High point: 3400 feet

Best: late spring but good all winter
Avalanche potential: low to
*   moderate*
Map: Green Trails, Kachess Lake

The Cooper River Road offers four different destinations, all with spectacular views of the Dutch Miller Gap peaks—Lemah Mountain, Chimney Rock, Overcoat Peak, Summit Chief, and Bears Breast Mountain.

Access: Drive from Roslyn toward Salmon la Sac (Tour 24) and 14.8 miles from Roslyn City Hall find Cooper River Road (2400 feet).

The road is groomed for snowmobiles and generally well packed and rutted. At 4¾ miles, gaining only 300 feet, the way reaches a major junction and the four alternatives.

Cooper Lake: Go right, downhill, ¼ mile and cross the Cooper River on a concrete bridge. Follow the road as it curves left another ¼ mile and

Lemah Mountain and Chimney Rock from Pete Lake ski route

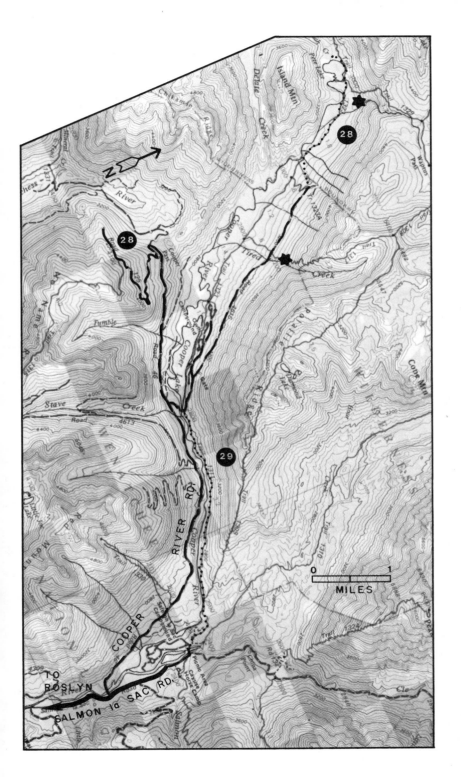

find a spur that drops to Owhi Campground and the lakeshore (2788 feet), 5½ miles from the beginning.

Cooper Pass: From the major junction go straight ahead, climbing clearcuts with fine views of Cooper Lake and the Dutch Miller Gap peaks. At 3 miles from the junction (7¾ miles from beginning) reach Cooper Pass (3400 feet). For better views go higher on one of the many logging roads on No Name Ridge. Cooper Pass is a great destination; unfortunately, it's great for snowmobiles also.

Tired Creek: Cross Cooper River (see Cooper Lake, above), keep right at the campground-lakeshore junction, and follow the road past Tired Creek to its very end at 3400 feet, 8½ miles from the Salmon la Sac Road.

This trip has excellent views of the Dutch Miller Gap peaks but crosses two avalanche gullies, so don't try it for a couple of weeks after a heavy snowstorm. If the avalanches have been massive enough, they will block the snowmobiles.

Pete Lake: This is the only place in the watershed where one can get away from machines and is recommended as an overnight trip for skiers with advanced-level skills and up. From the road-end beyond Tired Creek, traverse downward in a clearcut, then in forest, to the valley bottom and go upstream 2½ miles to Pete Lake and a great view of mountains (11 miles from the Salmon la Sac Road). The way through the forest is not easy when the snow is deep and there are "wells" around trees, or when it's not deep enough to bridge the half-dozen tributary streams. The route is subject to large avalanches, including an area just short of the lake.

CLE ELUM LAKE

29 COOPER RIVER TRAIL

Skill level: skilled intermediate
Round trip: 8 miles to Owhi Lake
  campground
Skiing time: 5 hours
Elevation gain: 400 feet

High point: 2900 feet
Best: January–February
Avalanche potential: low
Map: Green Trails, Kachess Lake

Map on page 83

Want to sneak away from the annoying whirl and whiz of pesky snowmobiles? The Cooper River Trail, wandering through the serene forests of the Salmon la Sac area, provides just such luxury. During the summer, two people can easily walk abreast along this broad trail, but winter snows transform this easy stroll into a challenging obstacle course. The trail narrows down to a thin thread, and skinny skis must be negotiated around tight switchbacks, between trees, and over deep tree wells, with

Cooper River Trail

lots of ups and downs. Better have good control of those boards if you don't intend to repeat Humpty Dumpty's great fall.

Access: Drive Interstate 90 to the Roslyn–Salmon la Sac Exit No. 80 and go northeast for 3 miles. Turn left on State Highway 903 and drive 17 miles to the Salmon la Sac Guard Station. The drivable road usually ends here.

The Tour: Ski past the guard station, then just before the main road to Fish Lake begins climbing, go left toward the campground. Ski across the Cle Elum River and turn right at the campground entrance gate. A few hundred feet farther a large Forest Service sign indicates the start of the Cooper River Trail No. 1311 and the Waptus River Trail No. 1310. Although the trails are all but invisible under the blanket of snow, follow a northwest bearing across the broad flats near the trailhead, heading away from the summer homes along the Cle Elum River and the Waptus River Trail on your right. As the terrain begins to rise, ski left along the base of a hill until reaching the Cooper River. If you are on the trail, you'll find summer homes on the left and forest on the right.

If the trail is not obvious, don't worry. Pick a route a couple of hundred feet away from the river and ski up the valley. By late February the trail becomes evident, but do not feel constrained to follow it. If the trail gets too close to the river, move uphill. If the trail makes a difficult creek crossing, find a better one.

After ¾ mile the Polallie Ridge Trail branches off. The Cooper River is now in a deep canyon and at 1½ miles the trail reaches its high point (2800 feet), avoiding steep walls near the river. The trail ends at Forest Road 4616 near Cooper Lake at 3½ miles. Turn right and follow snowmobile tracks for ½ mile to Owhi Campground with its lakeshore views. If you're still feeling spunky and want to log extra miles, see Tour 28.

Note: The Cooper River trailhead will be moved in the next few years. There will be plenty of signs at the old trailhead to direct you to the new.

30 TEANAWAY BUTTE

Skill level: intermediate
Round trip: 10 miles
Skiing time: 5 hours
Elevation gain: 2349 feet

High point: 4769 feet
Best: December–March
Avalanche potential: low
Map: Green Trails, Mount Stuart

If you like hard exercise, panoramic views, and fast-paced descents, Teanaway Butte is an ideal tour. The climb to the summit follows a steep logging road, guaranteed to give you a great workout. The views from the summit span the Cascades from Mount Stuart to Mount Rainier, an unbeatable combination on a clear day. And the descent is a mixture of open telemark slopes and a road that twists and rolls like corrugated aluminum.

Teanaway Butte is located on Boise Cascade land and the access road is closed to motorized vehicles. Despite the closure signs, numerous snowmobiles find their way into the area. To avoid these noisemakers, try visiting on a weekday.

Stuart Range viewed from the summit of Teanaway Butte

Access: Just east of Cle Elum, turn off Interstate 90 on Exit 85 and drive 7.6 miles toward Wenatchee on Highway 970. Turn left on Teanaway Road for 7.5 miles, then go left again on West Fork Teanaway Road. When the road divides in .7 mile, go right. Head up the Middle Fork Valley for 2.6 miles to the end of the county road and the end of the plowing (2420 feet). Park near the turnaround but out of the way of turning vehicles (that includes a school bus on weekdays).

The Tour: The first mile is an easy ski along the valley bottom. You'll probably meet snowmobiles in this section. Near ¾ mile pass a fish-screen station on the left. About 1000 feet beyond, look for the Teanaway Butte Road on the right, which starts in an open meadow. Ski across the meadow, past the Boise Cascade gate, then climb.

At 2½ miles (3380 feet) the road crests a broad, open ridge top with views of Yellow Hill to the west and Teanaway Butte with its three summits to the north. For the next ½ mile, ski along the crest of the ridge, descending to a narrow saddle before resuming the climb.

The first of many intersections occurs at 3½ miles, where the Teanaway Butte Road joins the Rye Creek Road. Most snowmobiles go right (downhill) to the North Fork Teanaway Road and 29 Pines Campground. Skiers should stay left and continue climbing. From this point on there are unsigned spur roads about every ¼ mile. However, if you go

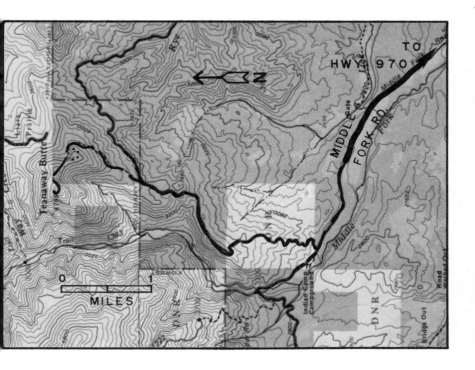

straight at every intersection you can't miss. The butte road climbs along the east side of a logged ridge for a mile, then bends west around the first of the three summits that comprise the butte.

For the best skiing, leave the road shortly after it turns west and climb to the top of the first summit. At the top you'll find perfect spots to sunbathe and tempting downhill runs on all sides except the west.

Skiers continuing on should follow the road to the saddle between the first and second summits. Stay to the right of the second summit and descend slightly to a saddle. Now the uphill slope steepens to the base of a small knoll at 5 miles. From here it may be best to remove the skis and posthole the final 200 feet to the narrow, rock-bound summit. Stay back from the edges, where large cornices frequently overhang on the north and west sides.

The summit of the butte is the site of a lookout, removed in 1968. Views are excellent in every direction, particularly to the north where the rocky ridges of Mount Stuart jab the skyline.

SWAUK CREEK

31 TEANAWAY RIVER AND BEAN CREEK BASIN

Teanaway River

Skill level: basic
Round trip: 4 miles or more
Skiing time: 2 hours or more
Elevation gain: 100 feet
High point: 2500 feet
Best: January–March
Avalanche potential: low
Map: Green Trails, Mount Stuart

Bean Creek Basin

Skill level: advanced
Round trip: 6 miles
Skiing time: 5 hours
Elevation gain: 2900 feet
High point: 6500 feet
Best: April
Avalanche potential: high
Map: Green Trails, Mount Stuart

Yes, the Teanaway River Road sees a lot of snowmobile traffic. Yes, the area has acquired a bad reputation among skiers. So do we recommend skiing here? Yes, yes, yes!

Despite the inconvenience of skiing among a gaggle of machines, midwinter skiing on the beautiful road bordering the Teanaway River can be a joy. You'll be treated to large scenic meadows, gently rolling terrain, and exhilarating views of the Stuart Range. And once the snow melts in the river valley it's time to put on the climbing skins and head up to the Bean Creek Basin high country for its outstanding telemark runs and panoramic views.

Access: To reach the Teanaway River area, drive 5 miles north from Interstate 90 on Highway 970, then turn west on Teanaway River Road. Fol-

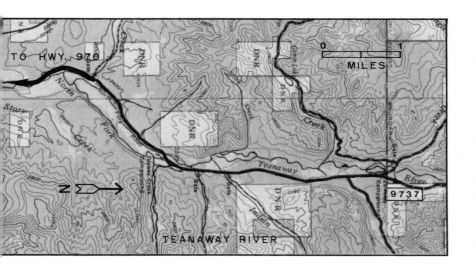

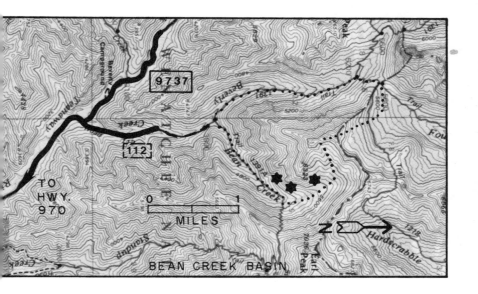

lowing the "North Fork Teanaway" drive 9 miles to the end of the plowed road (2500 feet), or onward to the snowline, wherever that is.

Because this is a low-elevation trip, the snowline fluctuates wildly—especially in December. If you drive beyond the end of the plowed road, be sure and get out fast if snow starts falling. No plows will come to rescue you and your vehicle beyond the Lick Creek turnoff.

Crossing Bean Creek

Teanaway River: From the snowplow turnaround, ski up the road paralleling the North Fork Teanaway River. After 1½ miles the road crosses the river, passes the Dickey Creek Campground, and heads through the first of a series of meadows. At 2 miles Mount Stuart and its satellites suddenly come into view. Take a good look, then continue on through the trees and more views for another ¾ mile.

At 4¼ miles the road divides at 29 Pines Campground (2500 feet). This makes a good turnaround point or overnight campsite. If you drove this far without encountering snow, take the right fork and continue up the valley toward Esmerelda Basin, where the skiing should be good.

Bean Creek Basin: To get to the excellent springtime backcountry skiing of Bean Creek Basin, drive the Teanaway River Road 13.2 miles to 29 Pines Campground. Go right for 3.9 miles on Road 9737 to the Beverly Creek Bridge. Just before crossing the creek, turn uphill on Road (9737)112 and drive 1.1 miles to the end of the road (3600 feet).

Start on the Beverly Turnpike Trail (an abandoned logging road), climbing through a clearcut for ¼ mile before reaching the actual trail. The trail climbs up the valley for 20 feet, then divides at Bean Creek. Turn right just before the creek and head uphill on the Bean Creek Trail.

Parallel Bean Creek, climbing steeply up a narrow valley for ¼ mile, before making a careful crossing over the creek. Climb up the slope into the trees, keeping the creek within hearing distance. Cross over two avalanche gullies before the valley bends sharply north entering lower Bean Creek Basin, 1½ miles from the car.

Here the valley opens up into wide meadows. Watch for avalanches from the rock walls above, especially after snowfall or during warm weather. Stay off the inviting slopes and ski up the valley bottom, paralleling Bean Creek. Follow the valley and creek as they bend east, then make a short and steep ascent to the upper basin. Continue east to the upper bowls and climb toward the summits at the valley head. Watch for cornices toward the ridge tops (6500 feet).

If you're game for more adventure and have a good map in tow, ski out of Bean Creek Basin into the Fourth Creek basin, over a 5600-foot saddle, and return to the car via the Beverly Turnpike Trail.

Upper end of Bean Creek Basin

32 RED TOP MOUNTAIN LOOKOVER

Skill level: intermediate
Round trip: 17 miles
Skiing time: 8 hours–2 days
Elevation gain: 2480 feet
High point: 5280 feet

Best: January–April
Avalanche potential: low
Maps: Green Trails, Liberty and Mt. Stuart

A high, open ridge gives panoramas out to Mount Stuart, Table Mountain, Mount Ingalls, Mount Rainier, and Mount Adams, and down to the Swauk and Teanaway valleys. Less than ½ mile away, perched high atop a rocky fortress, is Red Top Lookout, defended against skiers by snow- and ice-covered rock. The trip is long, requiring a full day or overnight. The first 6 miles are on well-graded logging roads made noisy and icy by snow-blitzers. The last 2½ miles are up an old skid road, then a trailless hillside, to a forested ridge top, very difficult to climb when icy.

Access: Drive Highway 97 east of Mineral Springs Resort (store-restaurant) .1 mile and turn off on Road 9701 at Blue Creek (2800 feet), the beginning point of this trip.

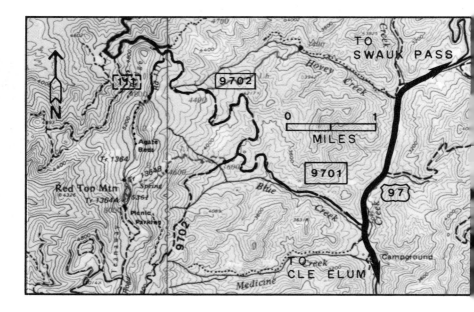

Red Top Lookout from the "Battlefield"

The Tour: At ½ mile from Highway 97, where Medicine Creek Road branches left, stay right. After the first mile Red Top Lookout, high above, makes an occasional appearance.

At a major intersection, 3 miles, a sign points left to Red Top Lookout. Stay right. At 6 miles is another junction at the top of a small saddle. Go left on an ill-defined skid road. Contour around the ridge to the road-end in a small, steep clearcut at 7 miles. From here climb to the ridge top. If the slope looks too steep or the snow unstable, backtrack ¼ mile to a small bend in the road and follow a gully to the ridge. Once on the crest continue south ½ mile through trees to the broad, open area of "The Battlefield," well known by the rockhounds who in summer dig pits and trenches, searching for agates. The winter restores peace, permitting skiers to serenely enjoy the views.

Iron Creek Road

33 IRON CREEK

Skill level: basic
Round trip: 6 miles
Skiing time: 3 hours
Elevation gain: 700 feet
High point: 3600 feet
Best: mid-December—mid-March
Avalanche potential: low
Map: Green Trails, Liberty

Ironically, in an area where snowmobiles are the dominant life form, Iron Creek Road provides sanctuary from the iron herd. Usually this road is snubbed by snowmobilers as unworthy of their mighty machines. As a result, the narrow little valley often offers families and beginning skiers a little piece of heaven.

Access: Drive 8.8 miles north along Highway 97 from the intersection of Highways 97 and 970 (or 7.8 miles west from Swauk Pass) to the Iron Creek road No. 9714. Park at a small pullout on the north side of the highway (2900 feet).

The Tour: Ski for ¼ mile along Iron Creek through a band of timber, then cross the creek as the valley opens (a good place for picnicking).

Continuing up the valley, the road wanders in and out of trees along the creek. After 1 mile, spur road (9714)112 branches left following the West Fork. This road was still under construction at the time of this writing (1987); however, intermediate-level skiers should enjoy skiing a secondary spur road branching off 1 mile up the West Fork and climbing steeply uphill to a viewpoint overlooking the Iron Creek area.

Following the Iron Creek road to the 2-mile mark, a second spur road (No. [9714]112) branches left. This road climbs steeply to a narrow pass 1 miles west of Blewett Pass (4000 feet), and is suitable for advanced-intermediate skiers when snow conditions are *very* stable.

Continuing up Iron Creek, a clearing at 2¾ miles suddenly reveals the end of the valley where the steep hillside rises to meet the summit of Teanaway Ridge. The road ends after 3 miles at the Iron Creek trailhead. The trail crosses several slide-prone hillsides and is not safe for winter travel. Turn around and enjoy the ride back down the valley.

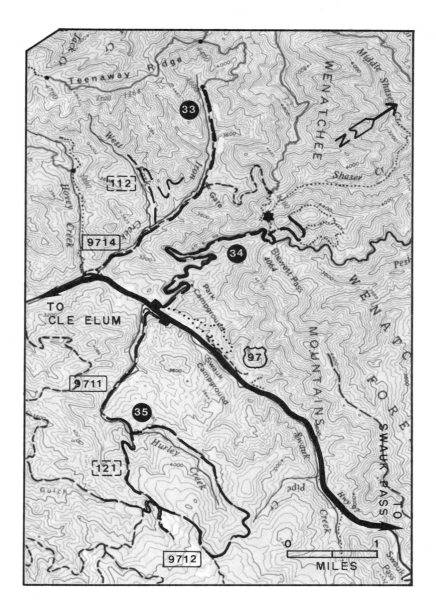

34 BLEWETT PASS

Blewett Pass

Skill level: advanced basic
Round trip: 8 miles
Skiing time: 4 hours
Elevation gain: 1030 feet
High point: 4064 feet
Best: January–March
Avalanche potential: low
Map: Green Trails, Liberty

Skiers' Trail

Skill level: advanced basic
Round trip: 2 miles
Skiing time: 1½ hours
Elevation gain: 250 feet
High point: 3300 feet
Best: January–February
Avalanche potential: none
Map: Green Trails, Liberty

Map on page 95

Old names never die.

Highway 97 moved from Blewett Pass to Swauk Pass over 25 years ago, but the new road is still referred to as the Blewett Pass Highway. This tour takes you along the real Blewett Pass Highway and is full of nostalgia—Model Ts used to chug and steam along here. Because old cars weren't going fast, the old road twisted and turned its way upward, following contours of the hillside and doubling back on itself at switchbacks. It's frightening just how narrow the old two-lane was. Views from the sharp switchbacks sweep down the Swauk River Valley to Red Top Mountain and snow-topped Teanaway Ridge, and the descent down the old highway is lots of fun, as long as you don't "lose your brakes" on the corners.

Access: Drive north on Highway 97 from Ellensburg or on Highway 970 from Cle Elum. At 7 miles from the junction of 97 and 970 pass Mineral Springs Resort. In 3 miles more find the old Blewett Pass Highway on the left (3048 feet). There is usually space for about four cars to park.

Blewett Pass: Two trails start from the parking area, one for skiers and one for snowmobilers. The snowmobilers' trail goes to Blewett Pass; the blue-diamonded Skiers' Trail does not. (Skiers' Trail is described below.)

Follow the orange diamonds straight up from the parking area. (Do not attempt to follow the snowmobile tracks; they go everywhere.) After 30 feet you will reach an obvious road. Go right and ski up the left side of a narrow clearing. Soon the timber closes in and the route is evident to the pass.

The grade is gentle but steady. As elevation is gained, Red Top Lookout can be seen to the southwest and the flat top of Table Mountain to the southeast. At 1 mile the road divides; the right fork goes to a campground area while the main road switchbacks up to the left.

At 4 miles (4064 feet), reach the summit of the pass. Nothing is there

Wenatchee Mountains viewed from Blewett Pass

now, but there used to be a small restaurant and, in the late 1930s, a rope-tow ski lift.

At the summit you are just a short distance from good views. Go left (west) and ski up a rough logging road, passing two spurs on the right. Stop at the edge of a long, open hillside and gaze down on the old highway below.

Skiers' Trail: If there are too many snowmobiles on the Blewett Pass Highway this alternate tour may save your day. It is a fun romp through the forest on a trail that gains very little elevation throughout the 2-mile tour. Best of all, the trail makes a loop so you won't have to keep dodging oncoming skiers.

The first half of the trail parallels the Swauk Pass Highway. The trail winds a bit from one old skid road to another, so pay close attention to the blue diamonds marking the route. Shortly after passing Swauk Pass Campground on the right, the route leaves the road, turns uphill, and bends back on itself.

The second half of the loop is considerably more challenging than the first. The return trip starts by wandering through the forest on a narrow trail, then climbs up an old streambed to an abandoned logging road. The route follows the logging road down. Near the bottom, it veers back into the forest for a run across an open hillside back to the parking area.

35 HURLEY CREEK LOOP

Skill level: intermediate
Round trip: 11 miles
Skiing time: 5 hours
Elevation gain: 1460 feet

High point: 4500 feet
Best: mid-December–mid-March
Avalanche potential: low
Map: Green Trail, Liberty

Map on page 95

With its easy climb, fast descent, open meadows, ideal length, and looping configuration, the Hurley Creek Loop could be one of the premier ski tours in the Swauk Pass area. Unfortunately, this road is groomed for snowmobile use even though parking is limited and there are numerous other snowmobile access points of greater popularity. The Hurley Creek area is yet another example of how we in the majority are trammeled by a minority who hold the purse strings. If you think it's unfair, write the Forest Service often and tell them to give skiers a fair share of roads. Tell them Hurley Creek Loop would make an excellent designated ski trail.

Until Armageddon delivers us from evil, ski the road early on weekends or on weekdays if you want to avoid the snowmobiles.

Access: Drive Highway 97 for 4.7 miles west from Swauk Pass (if coming from Highway 2) or 9.8 miles north from the intersection of Highways 97 and 970 (if coming from Interstate 90). Park on the south side of Highway 97 at the small Hurley Creek Road turnout (3040 feet), just opposite the old Blewett Pass Highway (Tour 34).

Mount Rainier seen from meadows on the Liberty-Beehive Road

Hurley Rock

The Tour: From the parking area, ski Road 9711 on a slightly descending course as it heads toward Hurley Creek. Near the creek the road makes an abrupt turn up the narrow valley and begins its steady climb. After ¾ mile the road crosses Hurley Creek and cuts through the first of two open meadows (excellent camping for those so inclined).

Recross Hurley Creek at 1¼ miles and climb past the next meadow. Near 2 miles the valley makes an abrupt 90-degree turn to the north. The walls close in and the road cuts into the hillside. The road enters Forest Service land after 2½ miles and spur road (9712)121 joins the main road on the right. This forms the return leg of the loop.

Continuing up Hurley Creek, the road passes Hurley Rock at 3 miles and gains a small saddle between Pipe Creek and Hurley Creek after 5 miles. Now the road swings south around the upper end of Hurley Creek.

Hurley Creek road ends at mile 6 (4500 feet) at the Liberty-Beehive road No. 9712—appropriately named for the swarm of buzzing snowmobiles you'll find here. Straight ahead is a beautiful meadow with an excellent view of Mount Rainier. Try a few turns here, and when you tire of playing slalom around the snowmobiles, head down Road 9712 for a steep mile. Pass two roads on the right (both lead to summer cottages) and at the third road (No. [9712]121) turn right. Following the road, cross the ridge and prepare yourself for a straight drop down to the Hurley Creek Valley at 8½ miles. The final 2½ miles are a pleasant glide back to the car.

A twisted tree on north side of
Swauk Pass

36 SWAUK PASS LOOPS

Skill level: basic
Round trip: 1–5 miles
Skiing time: 3 hours–all day
Elevation gain: up to 500 feet
High point: 4400 feet
Best: January–February
Avalanche potential: low
Map: Green Trails, Liberty

Deep in the heart of snowmobile country the Forest Service has reserved an area around Swauk Pass for travelers powered solely by bread, cheese, and enthusiasm. Although this area is not large, it is crisscrossed with so many trails that you can ski for an entire day without covering them all.

This is undoubtedly the best-developed "no fee" area set aside for skiers in the entire Washington Cascades. The Forest Service and local ski clubs deserve considerable approbation for the project, which includes marking of trails and the placement of numerous trail maps.

Access: Drive Highway 97 to Swauk Pass Summit (4102 feet), where Sno-Parks exist on both the north and south sides of the highway. Additional parking with access to the trails exists on the north side of the pass at .8 miles and 1.2 miles north of the summit.

The Tour: The best tours for beginners are the Tronson Meadows loops. Park on the east side of the highway .8 mile below the pass and ski the logging roads to the Practice Meadow, located 1½ miles from the highway. The meadows have a very gentle slope, just steep enough for beginners to practice. More advanced skiers will find challenge on the sections of trail connecting the roads. Side-Step Hill Trail leads to two open meadows steep enough to carve a long string of turns. Near the Practice Meadow, Tronson Meadow Trail climbs up to meet the Haney Meadow Trail. This provides intermediate skiers with a loop to Swauk Pass and back.

Opposite the highway from Tronson Meadows is the lower access to 2½ miles of trails on the north side of Swauk Pass. These loops start 1 mile below Swauk Pass at Tronson Campground. Park at the gated campground entrance and ski down into the snow-covered campsite loops. Beginners and snow players can make ½-mile loops through the camp area. Intermediate skiers will find a longer loop starting opposite the "Picnic Only" area. Head uphill to an open slope and climb to the top. Take a

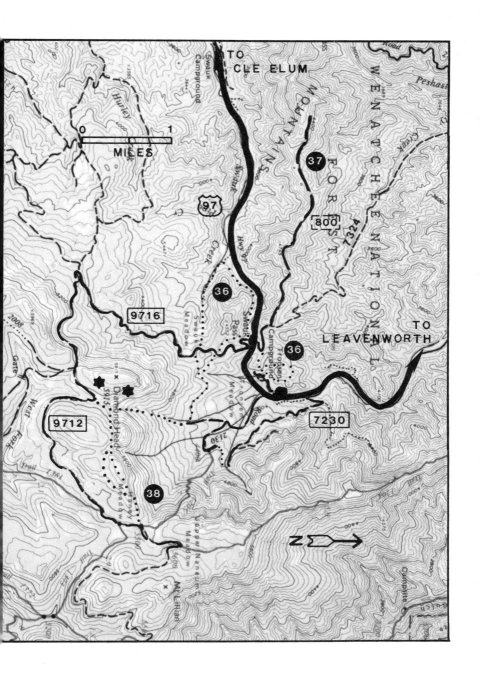

TO
CLE ELUM

WENATCHEE NATIONAL FOREST

Swauk Campground

Hurley

0   1
MILES

MOUNTAINS

WENATCHEE

37

FOREST

800

97

Swauk Creek

36

Swauk Pass

36

TO
LEAVENWORTH

9716

Tronsen Campground

9712

Diamond Head

Tronsen Meadow Road

7230

38

Upper Naneum Meadow

Mt. Lillian

N

Ski trail in Tronson Meadows area

skid road to the right and follow it to within 100 feet of the end. Climb uphill through a small basin and then up a rounded knoll to twisted trees and views of the Stuart Range. Ski left, back to the skid road, to complete the loop.

From the south-side Sno-Park at the summit of the pass, skiers can follow trails down to the Tronson Meadows area, ski the well-packed "shared corridor" (a logging road shared with snowmobiles), or take the challenging loop through Swauk Meadows. The loop through the meadows starts opposite the information board at the upper end of the Sno-Park. Ski across the top of the small snow-play area, then head steeply uphill on an old skid road. After ¾ mile, the trail reaches the "shared corridor"; go right on the road for ¼ mile to the top of a long open area. This is Swauk Meadows. Enjoy a long run down and at the bottom bear right into a second meadow. Follow blue diamonds into woods for an exhilarating run down a skid road. Then parallel the highway back to the Sno-Park.

The north-side Sno-Park serves as an alternate starting point for the ski loops originating at Tronson Campground. It also serves as a starting point for a "superloop" adventure which links the north-side trails to Tronson Meadows and Swauk Pass.

37 WENATCHEE RIDGE

Skill level: advanced basic
Round trip: 6 miles to road-end
Skiing time: 4 hours
Elevation gain: 458 feet
High point: 4560 feet

Best: January–February
Avalanche potential: low
Map: Green Trails, Liberty

Map on page 101

Ridge after ridge of gleaming, snow-covered hills, capped by Mount Adams, Mount Rainier, and Mount Stuart, are viewed from a top-of-the-world route along the crest of Wenatchee Ridge. If that isn't enough, the area has skiing for everyone from gung-ho 5-year-olds to their telemarking parents.

Access: Drive Highway 97 to Swauk Pass (4102 feet) and park in the north-side Sno-Park. A large Forest Service information and map board helps travelers orient themselves in the maze of roads.

The Tour: The road sets out east from the information board. Although most snowmobiles stay to the south side of the pass, expect to see a few in the first ½ mile. In 150 feet the road swings left (north) and the way to the Swauk Pass Loops (Tour 36) branches right, marked with bright blue

Stuart Range from Wenatchee Ridge Road

Skier on Wenatchee Ridge

triangles. Follow the road as it winds above the pass, gaining 200 feet in the first ½ mile, to reach a small pass and junction. Scotty Creek Road descends straight ahead into snowmobile country. Turn left on Wenatchee Ridge Road.

Unlike other ski trails in the Swauk Pass area, the ridge road soon breaks out of forest and the whole world opens up on either side. The way rolls along, dropping from the ridge top to contour around the higher peaks, then returning to the crest. Small knolls are scenic lunch spots as well as fun ski hills. Advanced skiers will find clearcut slopes of various steepness to challenge their turning abilities.

Save some energy for the road-end clearcut. Just before 3 miles the road splits. Climb the upper fork to the top of a small knoll for a final overlook of Red Top Mountain, the Swauk Valley, and lowlands beyond.

It is possible to follow the ridge another 2 miles to Blewett Pass, but as of this writing the forest was too dense to make the trip enjoyable.

38 HANEY MEADOW

Skill level: advanced
Round trip: 10 miles
  via trail route
Skiing time: 8 hours
Elevation gain: 1860 feet
High point: 5960 feet

Best: January–February
Avalanche potential: moderate
Map: Green Trails, Liberty

Map on page 101

Excellent snow and surprising views make the country around Haney Meadow a place for endless, happy hours on skis. The white meadow plain, ringed by forested hills, is a great base camp for days of exploring logging roads, trails, and ridge crests.

Access: Drive Highway 97 to Swauk Pass and park in the Sno-Park on the south side (4102 feet).

The Tour: There are two ways to Haney Meadow. One is the Table Mountain Road, which gets there in 10 comparatively gentle miles. It is easy to follow except near the Table Mountain turnoff, where it may be obscured by drifts of snow; in that case continue to contour and watch for silver markers on trees. This route is worth considering when snow is icy or avalanche hazard high. However, snow pilots abound on weekends, snarling and roaring, hitting speeds of 40 to 50 miles per hour, and open roads and meadows seem to bring out their kamikaze instincts.

The wise and quiet choice is the steep, rutted, and well-marked skier-only trail that leads to the meadow in 5 miles. The tour begins from the upper end of the Sno-Park and winds uphill for ½ mile on road shared with snowmobiles. The Haney Meadow Trail is the second ski trail branching off to the left. The trailhead is marked by a small metal sign nailed to a tree at the turnoff.

The trail starts off with a climbing traverse across a wide clearcut followed by a short descent and more climbing. At 1½ miles (4500 feet) from the Sno-Park the Tronson Meadow Ski Trail joins from the north. The Haney Meadow Trail continues straight ahead, settling down to the serious work of climbing a narrow valley on the east side of Diamond Head. Two open avalanche chutes are crossed. In time of snow-pack instability, detour off the trail, down into the cover of the trees below the chutes.

The trail ascends around the valley head and up open slopes on the far side. A tall, lone tree near the top marks another intersection at 4 miles (5840 feet). A 1-mile trail goes right to the Table Mountain razzers. The Haney Meadow Trail continues straight ahead to the forest edge, then turns right to climb up and down a knoll.

Sun filtering through the clouds on the Table Mountain road

At 4½ miles (5960 feet) the trail splits. Both forks lead to the meadows; the left is best for views. A short climb attains a ridge with a broad panorama of the Cascades, featuring the Stuart Range; this is the proper turnaround for day-tourers. The right fork traverses around the ridge to rejoin the left and the united way drops ½ mile to the end of an old spur road, which leads down 100 feet to the Table Mountain road. Turn right for the final short drop to Haney Meadow (5502 feet).

Are you camping? Include these in your day trips: Mount Lillian, Upper Naneum Meadows, Mission Ridge Ski Area via Road 9712, and Lion Rock via Road 3500, long but very scenic.

39 WHISTLER CREEK

Skill level: intermediate
Round trip: 4 miles
Skiing time: 2 hours
Elevation gain: 1200 feet
High point: 3600 feet

Best: mid-December–February
Avalanche potential: moderate
Map: Green Trails, Lester

It's sad when a tour's main selling point is not what it's got, but what it hasn't got. In the case of the Whistler Creek tour, what it doesn't have is too many snowmobiles. The reason? The road isn't long enough to attract many machines. It isn't long enough to attract marathon skiers, either, but it is just the ticket when weather or time mandates a short trip.

Access: Drive Highway 410 for 2 miles east of the little community of Greenwater, to Forest Road 70. Turn left and head up the Greenwater

Colquhoun Peak

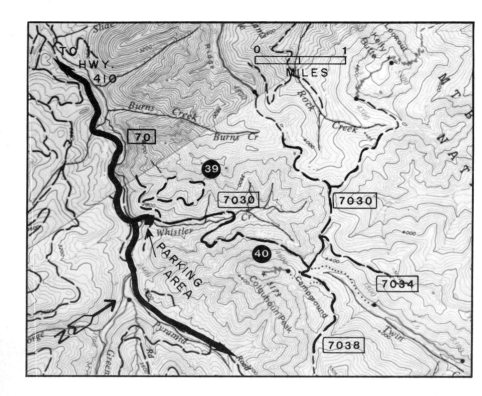

River road No. 70 for 7.8 miles before turning left on Road 7030. Drive another .2 mile to the Whistler Creek Sno-Park (2400 feet).

The Tour: From the Sno-Park ski ½ mile up Road 7030 (a snowmobile arterial up Whistler Creek). Turn uphill on a private logging road. At 1 mile keep right (the left fork climbs ⅛ mile, makes a sharp switchback, drops, and then dead-ends). The correct road drops a few feet, then starts climbing again. At all future junctions, take the uphill choice. Road's end is reached at 2 miles (3600 feet).

Here you'll find an impressive viewpoint overlooking Whistler Creek and the Greenwater River. In the distance Mount Rainier looks like a titanic scoop of vanilla ice cream, rising above the many.

40 TWIN CAMP

Skill level: intermediate
Round trip: 7 miles or many more
Skiing time: 4 hours or more
Elevation gain: 1900 feet

High point: 4300 feet
Best: mid-December—mid-April
Avalanche potential: low
Map: Green Trails, Lester

Map on page 108

Twin Camp—it's in the heart of Snowmobiling Country. Upon leaving the Sno-Park (established with snowmobile *and* skier funds) you'll ski up an icy road marred by tread marks that pitch you either on your nose or on your can. Sounds fun so far?

Lunch stop on Sawmill Ridge

No? So did we include this tour simply to add bulk to the book? No! We included this tour because we wanted to get up on our soapbox. It is strange that no designated ski trails exist in the Greenwater drainage. Perhaps this discrimination is an accidental oversight on the part of the Forest Service, so write them a letter and share your opinions. Be counted. We don't think it's reasonable or safe for skiers to share the road with snowmobiles speeding along at 40 mph.

We also included this tour because it's pleasant during the midweek or when thaws soften the snow pack enough to bog down the noisy machines. At such times the Twin Camp area is beautiful. Roads branch in multiple directions allowing for days of exploration. From the forested ridge tops you can ski down sparsely wooded slopes overlooking Tacoma's Green River watershed (shed your water on the opposide side to keep the watershed pure) or gaze over clearcut ridges at the snowy mass of Mount Rainier.

Access: Drive Highway 410 east 2 miles from the Greenwater General Store. Just before the overpass, turn left on Forest Road 70. Go 7.8 miles, then turn left again on Forest Road 7030. Drive .2 mile to the Whistler Creek Sno-Park or to the snowline.

The Tour: Ski along Whistler Creek on Road 7030 for 1 mile, then cross the creek (staying right at the fork) and climb steadily through a very bare clearcut. Switchback into forest and at 3 miles reach the ridge and a four-way intersection (4100 feet).

Now the choices. Road 7038, the right fork, climbs for ½ mile around the forested flanks of Colquhoun Peak to Twin Camp Campground, a natural turnaround point. The hyperactive and those with more than one day to spend can continue on past the camp for 8 more miles of rolling ridge tops with excellent vantage points. Road 7030, the left fork, is not groomed for snowmobiles and becomes a haven for skiers with several possible destinations: follow Road 7030 for 3 more miles to its end on Huckleberry Mountain, 6 miles from the Sno-Park; or ski Road 7030 for ½ mile beyond the intersection, then head uphill at the first junction on the Sawmill Ridge road No. 7034 for 1 mile to its end at 4800 feet, 4½ miles from the Sno-Park.

41 HUCKLEBERRY RIDGE

Skill level: intermediate
Round trip: 8 miles or more
Skiing time: 4 hours
Elevation gain: 1577 feet
High point: 3520 feet
Best: mid-December–March

Avalanche potential: low
Maps: USGS and Green Trails,
* Greenwater*

Here's an area of almost unlimited potential for plodders, swooshers, racers, and trail breakers. This subalpine ridge sports miles and miles of crewcut hills as well as a mind-boggling network of roads. The results of all this human handiwork are far-flung views and roads to anywheresville. Meanwhile, skiers sure of their map-reading and skiing skills can skim across the clearcuts and develop their own paths along the ridge crest. Best of all, there aren't that many snowmobiles in this area.

Access: Drive Highway 410 east 3.6 miles from the Greenwater General Store. Turn right on Forest Road 74 for .4 mile, then left on Road 75. Go less than .1 mile and make another left turn, still on Road 75 (1943 feet),

Skiers on Huckleberry Ridge Road

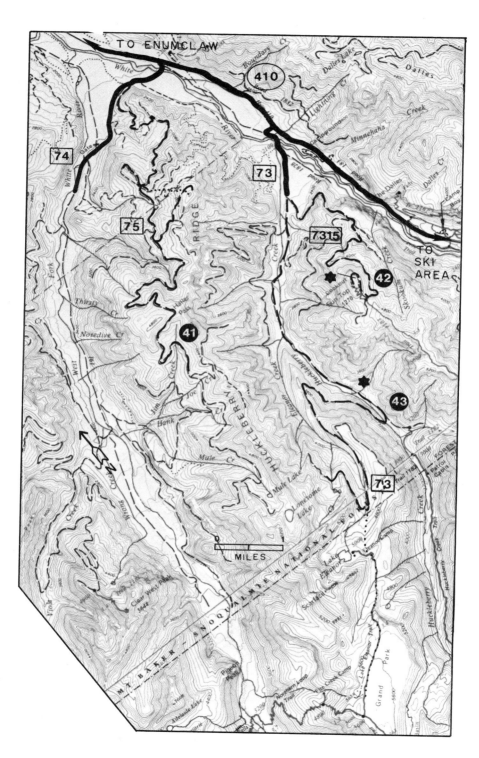

and head uphill to the snow. There is no Sno-Park, so be sure to park out of the way of local traffic and driveways.

The Tour: Follow Road 75 as it climbs steadily through the forest for 2 miles. The first viewpoint at 2¼ miles looks out over the White River to Dallas Ridge. The next viewpoints look west over the West Fork White River.

At 3½ miles (3300 feet), reach a four-way intersection. Skiers who feel droopy should turn right and then immediately turn right again. Climb steeply ⅛ mile to an old logging platform on the hilltop for a 360-degree view complete with Mount Rainier hovering above Huckleberry Ridge.

Perky skiers have a multitude of options. From the four-way intersection head up the clearcut hill for 1 mile. Cross three logging roads and at the fourth go left for views to the south and east.

The truly hyperactive may make a loop using Roads 75 and 74, skiing over 4650-foot Haller Pass and returning along the West Fork White River for a 15-mile total. This loop is only possible during midwinter when the snow is thick in the valley bottoms, and four-wheel-drive vehicles are unable to rut the snow on the West Fork Road.

WHITE RIVER

42 SUN TOP LOOKOUT

Skill level: intermediate
Round trip: 10–11 miles
Skiing time: 6 hours
Elevation gain: 2180 or 3030 feet to the summit
High point: 4420 or 5279 feet at the summit

Best: December–March
Avalanche potential: low to saddle, high at summit
Map: Green Trails, Greenwater

Map on page 112

Without any intended reference to Barbra Streisand records, on a clear day you really can see forever from atop Sun Top Lookout. You'll see the snowy slopes of Mount Baker, Glacier Peak, Mount Stuart, the Olympics, Mount Rainier—and that's only the beginning. Carry a map to identify the scores of other spires and bumps that rise around you.

Many highs have a corresponding low, and that is the case with this tour and the prolific snowmobile use of this area. The road to the saddle below Sun Top summit is groomed for skiers, but snowmobile use is not restricted so do not expect to find good ski tracks. Sometimes you've just got to take the lumps.

Access: Drive Highway 410 east from Enumclaw 24.2 miles and turn right on Huckleberry Creek road No. 73. The road should be plowed for 1.5 miles to the Sno-Park (2240 feet).

Mount Rainier viewed from below the summit of Sun Top

The Tour: Ski about 200 feet from the Sno-Park on Road 73, turn left, and head uphill on Road 7315. The climb is steady and the road slips rapidly through a green-and-white patchwork of forest and clearcut, passing an occasional spur road. Spur road (7315)301 branches to the right, offering views over Huckleberry Creek, and ½ mile farther spur road (7315)401 branches to the left, ending in a clearcut overlooking the White River Valley.

At about 5 miles, the road makes a final switchback to the 4420-foot saddle below Sun Top. The groomed trail ends here, and on most days so does the tour. Between the saddle and the summit the road crosses several extremely dangerous avalanche slopes. Most of the views seen from the summit can be found by continuing on Road 7315 to the vantage points of Mount Rainier in the clearcuts beyond.

For those choosing to continue to the summit of Sun Top despite the very real hazard of avalanches, take spur road (7315)501 up from the saddle to the edge of the trees, then ski or hike directly up the south rib to the lookout, following the summer trail. Do not ski the road beyond the edge of the trees as both the east and west sides of the summit pyramid are extremely hazardous. After heavy snowfalls no route to the summit is safe and skiers of all skill levels should turn back at the saddle.

114

43 GRAND PARK

Skill level: intermediate
Round trip: 21 miles
Skiing time: 2–3 days
Elevation gain: 3540 feet
High point: 5640 feet
Best: January–March
Avalanche potential: moderate
Maps: Green Trails, Greenwater
 and Mount Rainier East

Map on page 112

As a rule most winter tours on the flanks of Mount Rainier National Park are strictly reserved for competent ski mountaineers. But most rules have their exceptions, and strong skiers with 2–3 days can attain the wide meadows of Grand Park, just a stone's throw from the northeast base of "The Mountain." Unfortunately, the access road may be cluttered with machinery on weekends.

Access: Drive to the Sun Top Mountain Sno-Park (2240 feet; see Tour 42).

The Tour: Join the snowmobile parade and ski up Road 73, passing several spurs that are excellent for day touring. After a mile in the trees the road enters the clearcut Huckleberry Creek Valley and parallels the creek. At 4 miles cross a narrow avalanche chute. The chute slides early in the season and at regular intervals thereafter. Be cautious here at all times and particularly so during or just after heavy precipitation.

At 4½ miles the road crosses Huckleberry Creek (2960 feet). From the crossing the road gains elevation quickly for 1½ miles, then at the 3680-foot level bends sharply into the Eleanor Creek drainage. The grade now gentles. After another 2 miles the road bends sharply to cross Eleanor Creek (4480 feet). Leave the road, and the snow machines, and enter the forest left (east) of Eleanor Creek. In a few yards you'll cross the park boundary. The protection of the park and the trees makes a fine location for base camp.

The next 3 miles are an unmarked route through the trees to Grand Park. From the National Park boundary head south-southwest, keeping to the left of the small valley between Scarface to the west and the ridge to the east. If you come to Lake Eleanor, you have gone too far up the next valley.

Grand Park and Mount Rainier from Scarface

The route gradually gains elevation until ¼ mile before it enters Grand Park. Here climb steeply for 200 feet to the flat meadowland with broad views of the Carbon, Winthrop, and Emmons glaciers. After your eyes weary of our state's greatest heap of snow, look away, to lower peaks, to snow-hung trees, and to the critter tracks on the glistening white plain.

116

44 BUCK CREEK TOUR

Skill level: basic
Round trip: up to 10 miles
Skiing time: up to 5 hours
Elevation gain: 1800 feet

High point: 4400 feet
Best: mid-December–March
Avalanche potential: moderate
Map: Green Trails, Greenwater

We headed out to find a tour in the White River Valley away from snowmobiles and we found a real gem at Buck Creek. This area is a wintering ground for elk and is closed from November through April to all motorized use. On this tour you can count on seeing elk sign (tracks winding up and down the hillsides) as well as views over the White River Valley. The tour follows a road for 5 miles, winding in and out of the Buck Creek drainage, ending at the top of a clearcut on a flank of Fawn Ridge. However, there is no need to ski the entire distance to enjoy the views, which are as good at 1½ miles as they are at the top.

Access: Drive to Enumclaw and then east on Highway 410 to Greenwater. From the Greenwater General Store continue 11.5 miles, then turn right opposite the large Forest Service "Organizational Sites" sign. Cross the White River and continue on for .2 mile to a fork and go right on Road 7160. In .9 mile a large sign marks the entrance to the Buck Creek Church Camp. If there is room to park on the left side of the road, just before the

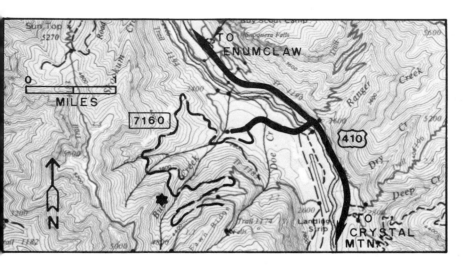

Buck Creek Road

sign, do so; if not, drive the .9 mile back to the intersection, park, and return on skis along the edge of the road.

The Tour: Buck Creek Road begins directly in front of the church camp sign (2600 feet), heading across the valley floor for ⅛ mile before starting to climb. A spur road joins on the left at the first switchback. At ½ mile the road divides (no road signs); take the right fork to cross Buck Creek, then climb into an open clearcut and views. To the east Snoquera Falls makes its breathtaking plunge down a broad expanse of cliffs; south lie the snowcapped summits of Castle Mountain, Norse Peak, and Crystal Mountain, and right below is the forested White River Valley.

The road climbs across the clearcut, switchbacks, and heads over the top of the clearing. At 2 miles is a gate; ski around it and continue the climb. At 3¼ miles the road divides (this should be the turnaround point if there has been any recent snowfall). Take the right fork and descend across an avalanche slope, cross Buck Creek for a second time, then resume the climb. At 4 miles the road enters a large clearcut. The final mile of the tour is spent switchbacking up to the logging platform at the top of the clearing.

45 CORRAL PASS

Skill level: intermediate
Round trip: 10 miles
Skiing time: 6 hours
Elevation gain: 3000 feet
High point: 5700 feet

Best: December–mid-May
Avalanche potential: low
Maps: Green Trails, Mount Rainier
East, Greenwater, and Lester

Here's a day tour for all seasons—be it late fall, midwinter, or early spring. But don't limit your explorations of the Corral Pass environs to day use only. High ridge tops and snowy bowls abound in the area, making the pass a fine overnight destination as well.

The Corral Pass Road starts at 2700 feet and climbs, climbs, and then climbs some more. In 5 miles, 3000 feet of elevation are gained. Start at

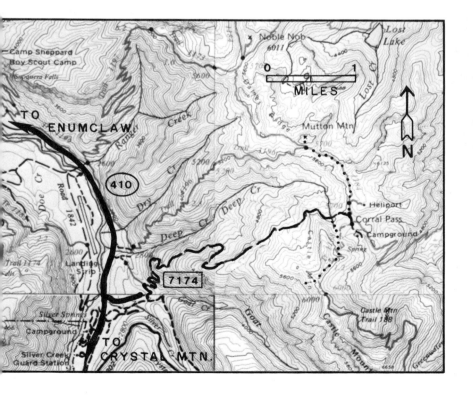

Ski route from Corral Pass to Mutton Mountain, Mount Rainier in distance

the bottom with a fast stride and hope that the momentum will carry on to the top.

Access: Drive Highway 410 from Enumclaw east through Greenwater and on. Note the mileage as you pass the Four Season Mountain Resort and continue east for .5 mile to the Corral Pass road No. 7174 on the left-hand side of the highway. In midwinter parking is difficult. There is no parking on the Corral Pass Road unless the snow level lies above 3000 feet, well above the cluster of private cabins. The closest parking in this case is at the Silver Springs Sno-Park, .4 mile past the Corral Pass Road on Highway 410.

The Tour: When the snow level is down to Highway 410, walk from the Sno-Park back to the Corral Pass Road. Walk up this road for ½ mile past vacation cabins to an intersection. Skiing will start here (2850 feet). Continue straight on Road 7174 and climb. Steep switchback follows steep switchback until you arrive at an open meadow below Castle Mountain (5300 feet) after 4¼ miles. If time allows, ski the delightful slopes at the south and southwest end of the meadow on an offshoot ridge of Castle Mountain.

Corral Pass is reached at 5 miles (5700 feet). Ski right at the pass to find a large open area, parking lot, summertime picnic area, and winter campsite. For an alternative campsite, continue along the road to the Corral Pass Campground, located on a small, frozen stream running through the trees.

If time allows ski north from the pass to Mutton Mountain. There is a trail from the pass but it offers poor skiing, so stick to the ridge tops. From the open area at the pass, ski straight east to the hillside and climb up through a band of trees. At the first open area turn north and climb up to the ridge top. Continue north over several small rolls along the ridge until it drops off in front of your skis. Descend to the west to a saddle, then climb to rounded Mutton Mountain (5900 feet). If you got this far without noticing the view, now is the time to feast your eyes. Mount Rainier fills the horizon to the southwest, while Mount Stuart and the Snoqualmie-area peaks rise to the east. Finally, Noble Knob to the north and Castle Mountain to the south scratch the sky as well.

WHITE RIVER

46 NORSE PEAK

Bullion Basin

Skill level: mountaineer
Round trip: 4 miles
Skiing time: 3 hours
Elevation gain: 1500 feet
High point: 5700 feet
Best: mid-December–May
Avalanche potential: moderate
Map: Green Trails, Bumping Lake

Norse Peak

Skill level: mountaineer
Round trip: 9 miles
Skiing time: 6 hours
Elevation gain: 2656 feet
High point: 6856 feet
Best: mid-December–May
Avalanche potential: high
Map: Green Trails, Bumping Lake

Bullion Basin and Norse Peak are perfect examples of the challenging backcountry skiing found in the Crystal Mountain area. The mountains rise straight out of the valley floor and avalanches commonly sweep their slopes. Skiers unable to assess avalanche danger are playing a game of

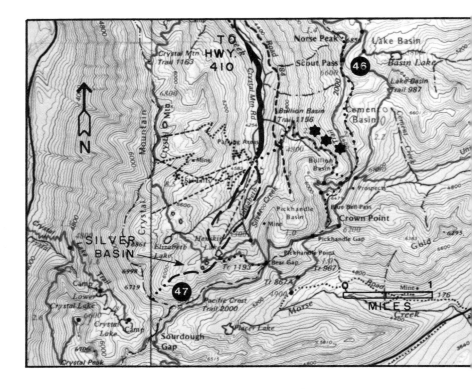

Russian roulette stepping out on these slopes. But experienced skiers who know when the slopes are safe can knock the needle off the fun meter, cranking tight turns down the long bowls.

Bullion Basin is a mere scoop cut into rugged talus. Sheltered by shady nooks and crannies, the snow stays light and powdery here long after elsewhere it has turned to corn or melted. Do not ski above Bullion Basin except when the snow pack is very stable.

Norse Peak lies above Bullion Basin, above timberline, and above the avalanches that plague the steep hillsides around it. Start the tour early so you'll have ample time to sample the bowls just beyond Norse Peak.

Access: Drive Highway 410 east from Enumclaw to the gated entrance of Mount Rainier National Park. Turn left and drive to the end of the Crystal Mountain Road and the downhill skiers' parking area (4200 feet). Register with the Ski Patrol and get the latest update on avalanche conditions.

The Tour: Bullion Basin and Norse Peak tours start from the top of Chair 7. Skiers not riding up on the lift should head up the Blue Bell Run, starting just to the right of the chair, and climb to the chair's uppermost terminal (5100 feet).

Skier below Bullion Basin

Two routes lead on to the basin and peak. On the left side of the valley a steep jeep road cuts an obvious path, but this area is extremely avalanche-prone and should mostly be avoided. The safest route is to the right, climbing to the top of a sparsely timbered knob behind the chair. Keep right along the valley wall in level terrain until the slope steepens, then enter dense timber. At 5500 feet cross the first of several small clearings. Bullion Basin lies only 200 vertical feet above, but it requires ¼ mile of climbing through sparse forest on either side of a prominent knob to reach it. Above the knob climb through a final fringe of timber to the 5700-foot bowl at the head of Bullion Basin.

To reach Norse Peak follow the edge of the timber north around the entrance to the 5700-foot bowl, then head up a sparsely timbered ridge to a 6700-foot knoll. In the next 1½ miles ski over the knoll and head north along the ridge overlooking Cement Basin, over a second 6700-foot knoll, and along the ridge at the top of Lake Basin, to the 6856-foot summit of Norse Peak.

If time and weather permit, ski the sweeping slopes of Lake Basin and Big Crow Basin on the east side of the peak.

47 SILVER BASIN

Silver Basin

Skill level: advanced
Round trip: 4½ miles
Skiing time: 4 hours
Elevation gain: 1800 feet
High point: 6000 feet
Best: mid-December–May
Avalanche potential: low
Map: Green Trails, Bumping Lake

Bear Gap

Skill level: advanced
Round trip: 4½ miles
Skiing time: 4 hours
Elevation gain: 1682 feet
High point: 5882 feet
Best: mid-December–March
Avalanche potential: low
Map: Green Trails, Bumping Lake

Map on page 122

Completely hidden from the noise and hard-packed slopes of the Crystal Mountain Ski Area, Silver Basin lies secluded by steep mountain walls in a fairy-tale world of winter beauty. Deep, fluffy powder often covers the small lakes, open meadows, and hillsides, offering a variety of skiing from serene gliding to mad downhill thrills. Bear Gap gives untracked snow and views to corniced ridges and snowbound Cascade Mountains.

Access: Park at the Crystal Mountain Ski Area parking lot (Tour 46) (4200 feet). Be sure to register with the Ski Patrol and check on avalanche conditions before starting out.

Silver Basin: The first 1000 feet to Silver Basin can be gained by skiing up the Quicksilver Run (climbing skins will help) or riding Chair 4. From the chair top (5420 feet), a snow cat often sets a track to Silver Basin. If no track can be seen, head southwest toward Hen Skin Lake, reached in ½ mile. Circle the east shore and proceed west, continually gaining elevation. Another long ¼ mile passes two more small, snow-covered lakes to an open meadow (5580 feet). Follow this long clearing southwest into Silver Basin. The wide-open slopes above are prime cross-country downhilling terrain. If snow conditions are stable, ski up to the ridge for a breathtaking view of Mount Rainier.

The return retraces the route to the top of Chair 4, then takes one of the downhill runs to the bottom. The Tinkerbell Run to the left (west) of Quicksilver is suggested since it usually is the least mogulled.

Bear Gap: From the parking lot ski up the Boondoggle Run or ride Chair 4 and ski to the southeast end of Boondoggle (5460 feet). Head southeast in untracked snow, aiming for the lowest saddle in the ridge, Bear Gap (5882 feet), a long ¾ mile from the top of Chair 4. Cross the gap to views south and east, the perfect lunch spot on a sunny day. The return to Chair 4 is a long, rolling downhill run.

Excellent skiing near Bear Gap

48 CHINOOK PASS AND NACHES PEAK

Chinook Pass

Skill level: intermediate
Round trip: 4 miles
Skiing time: 2 hours
Elevation gain: 832 feet
High point: 5432 feet
Best: November–December
Avalanche potential: low
Maps: Green Trails, Mount Rainier
East; USGS, Chinook Pass

Naches Peak (false summit)

Skill level: advanced
Round trip: 7 miles
Skiing time: 4 hours
Elevation gain: 1760 feet
High point: 6360 feet
Best: November–December
Avalanche potential: moderate
Maps: Green Trails, Mount Rainier
East and Bumping Lake;
USGS, Chinook Pass

Skiing in the Chinook Pass–Naches Peak area starts with the first major snowstorms to hit the Cascades. There is great fun to be had challenging the open bowls leading to Dewey Lakes or simply taking in incomparable views of Mount Rainier.

The skiing season around Chinook Pass starts and ends early. Beginning as soon as Highway 410 is closed over the pass, it ends when 4694-foot Cayuse Pass is snowed in, usually by mid- to late-December. In late spring there is often another week or two of skiing before the snowplows come to end the fun.

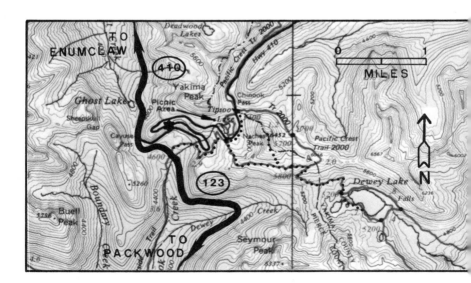

Mount Rainier from a shoulder of Naches Peak

No entry up closed Highway 410 is recommended during midwinter. There are several steep avalanche slide areas along the roadway, making travel extremely hazardous.

Chinook Pass: From Enumclaw drive Highway 410 for 41 miles to the summit of Cayuse Pass and park. Do not, under any circumstances, walk or ski the road as it is extremely prone to avalanches.

On skis, contour through the trees below the Chinook Pass Highway heading southeast for ¼ to ½ mile, before heading uphill. Be sure to stay well away from the highway and in the protection of the trees. After ½ mile of climbing steeply, the forest route bisects the highway where it makes a sharp switchback north. Follow the creek or the road to reach 5294-foot Tipsoo Lake and excellent views of Mount Rainier from the snowbound bowl. The road can be followed for the final ½ mile to Chinook Pass. Skiing beyond the pass is not recommended as the steep slopes are avalanche-prone.

Naches Peak (the false summit): From Tipsoo Lake, follow the road another 500 feet and climb to the smaller Tipsoo Lake. Then ski south up a lightly timbered ridge. When the open slope below a ridge running west from the false summit of Naches Peak is reached, traverse west in order to gain the ridge, avoiding the cornices above. Once on the ridge crest, follow its south side to the false summit of Naches Peak, the 6360-foot chief viewpoint of the trip. From the false summit, ski out to Dewey Lakes or just be satisfied with a great run back to the car. Sections of the descent are steep so be sure your turns and stopping ability are in good form.

Bridge over American River at Pleasant Valley Campground

49 PLEASANT VALLEY LOOP

Skill level: advanced basic
Round trip: 7 miles
Skiing time: 4 hours
Elevation gain: 400 feet

High point: 3600 feet
Best: January–mid-March
Avalanche potential: none
Map: Green Trails, Bumping Lake

Sandwiched between steep walls of the Fifes Peaks and American Ridge, Pleasant Valley melts out slower than surrounding ridges. The Forest Service has developed a 6-mile cross-country loop that allows skiers to take advantage of the lingering snow while skimming along a tree-lined trail. The two legs of the loop, on opposite sides of American River, differ radically. The southeast leg follows a narrow trail along a rolling hillside, suitable for intermediate skiers or better. The northwest side follows a skid road which is wide, open, and nearly level the whole distance—good skiing for everyone.

The loop lies between Hells Crossing Campground and Pleasant Valley Campground. There is parking at each place. Upriver from Pleasant Valley Campground are 4 more miles of loop trail.

Access: From the intersection of Highways 410 and 12, drive 33.3 miles toward Chinook Pass on 410 to Hells Crossing Campground and park in the small turnout provided (3280 feet). The alternate start is at Pleasant Valley Campground, 3.3 miles farther. Be sure to carry chains and shovel at all times on this road; it is plowed on a low-priority basis, once a week at most.

The Tour: To do the full loop from Hells Crossing Campground, begin with the southeast leg, climbing above the American River. Starting just before the highway bridge, the trail ascends in sight and sound of the rushing river, then enters a forest world stilled in winter except for an occasional breeze or the call of a lonely bird impatient for spring. The ascent yields to a roller-coaster path through tall pines. Occasional windows in the forest open out on the rugged Fifes Peaks to the north. At 3 miles descend back to the river. At 100 feet before the bridge a trail branches left up the valley, in 2 more scenic miles meeting Highway 410. (This trail is part of another loop; see map.)

The loop trail crosses the American River, passes through Pleasant Valley Campground, and crosses the highway (3440 feet). A short climb through trees reaches the skid road, an easy slide back down the valley. This leg has no scenic viewpoints but plenty to see; compare nature's handiwork to man's as the road passes from virgin forest to selectively logged areas. The loop is closed at 5 miles. Ski through Hells Crossing Campground and thence to the starting point.

New trails are being added to this area all the time. First-time skiers may enjoy exploring the new trail on the north side of Highway 410 starting at Hells Crossing and ending at Miner Creek (not surveyed by the authors).

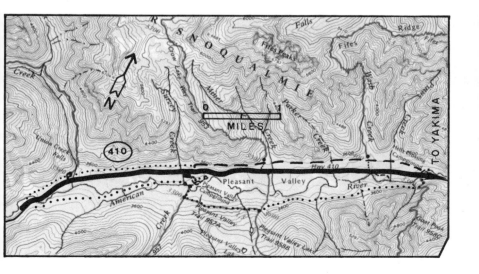

50 ALMOST A LOOP OF BUMPING LAKE

Skill level: basic
Round trip: up to 12 miles
Skiing time: 1–6 hours
Elevation gain: none

High point: 3460 feet
Best: January–February
Avalanche potential: low
Map: Green Trails, Bumping Lake

In the early 1980s Bumping Lake Reservoir was nearly overrun by snowmobilers who scared skiers away to more congenial areas. But in 1984, the creation of the William O. Douglas Wilderness closed the hills around the lake to all forms of motors. While the lake and adjacent logging roads remain open, snowmobiles are no longer free to roam the ridge tops and tend to avoid the area altogether. Don't feel too sorry for the gas guzzlers, as they still have all of the Little Naches as well as the Naches River area for their playground. Meanwhile, skiers are slowly rediscovering the Bumping Lake area.

Snow-covered tree stumps at Bumping Lake Reservoir

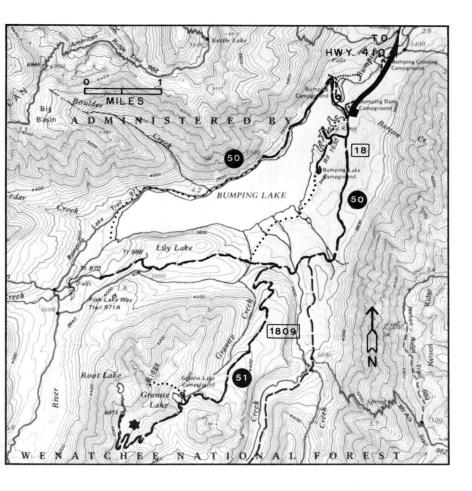

The reservoir's lower water levels in winter expose a broad, open shore between the lake and forest that is ideal for skiing. You'll find long level sections for gliding, short descents for practice turning, and delightful views of the surrounding wilderness.

In theory it is possible to ski all the way around the lake on the shore area. In reality two obstacles interfere: the Bumping River at the southwest end of the lake, and a steep hill on the southeast side. So instead of one long loop, we suggest you try two shorter loops.

Access: Drive the Bumping River road to its end (3460 feet). (See Tour 51 for directions.)

The Tour: For the first loop, ski north from the parking area across the dam. On the far side, follow the summer road to the left through trees for

1½ miles. Pass the marina and a group of summer cottages. When the road ends, ski down to the shore on the lake trail. Go left and ski back to the dam along open shore, playing slalom between the snow-crested stumps. Avoid skiing on the lake. No matter how solid it may appear, thin spots in the ice are common, especially near the dam. For those wishing to go farther, ski the shoreline for 3 miles from the road's end to the Bumping River at the far end of the lake.

The second loop starts from the parking area and follows Forest Road 18 on the east side of the lake. At ¼ mile ski to the right on the Boat Ramp road and descend gently toward the shore. Near the lake turn left and ski ½ mile to Bumping Lake Campground. Ski the campground loop, then descend to the open shoreline and ski back to the dam and parking area along the edge of the lake.

AMERICAN RIVER

51 MINERS RIDGE

Skill level: intermediate
Round trip: 17 miles
Skiing time: 8 hours
Elevation gain: 2612 feet
High point: 6072 feet

Best: mid-December–April
Avalanche potential: moderate
Map: Green Trails, Bumping Lake

Map on page 131

When it comes to views, Miners Ridge is like a scantily clad sex symbol who luxuriates in teasing admirers. There is almost a view of Mount Rainier, almost a view of Bumping Lake, almost a view of American Ridge, and almost a view of Nelson Ridge. But a thin veil of trees hides the wares. Not until you've gone the full 8 miles and reached the summit of Miners Ridge does the tease relent and show you a sight for sore eyes—a full panoramic display of peaks. The anticipation makes the view all the more special.

Access: Drive Highway 12 to the Highway 410 turnoff and head up the Naches River Valley and then the American River Valley for 28.5 miles. Turn left at the Bumping River Road turnoff and drive to the parking area (usually another 11 miles) at the end of the plowed road (3460 feet).

The Tour: Start by skiing up the east side of Bumping Lake on Forest Road 18, admiring the towering summits of Nelson Ridge, almost visible through the trees. This first section of the tour is fairly level and the miles tick off rapidly on a road smoothed by frequent snowmobile use.

The first major intersection occurs at 2½ miles; go right, still on Road 18. At 3 miles comes a second junction (3580 feet). Turn left on Miners Ridge road No. 1809 and shed a layer of clothing in anticipation of the work to come. Now climb steadily, making several switchbacks before easing off on the broad crest of a densely forested ridge. Take time during the climb to enjoy the almost-view of Mount Rainier and to study the snow-measuring equipment on the left side of the road.

Just when it appears the road will dead-end into a steep hillside, the route swings west, following a climbing traverse up to Granite Lake and Campground at 6½ miles (5060 feet). The lake and campground offer an enjoyable place to camp. They also mark the turnoff for those who would enjoy skiing untracked slopes to the ridge top. The route is simple: stay to the northeast end of the lake and follow the trees to the top of the ridge.

Beyond the lake the road climbs to a small pass, then takes a nearly level, mile-long traverse south, entering into a zone of potential avalanche hazard along some steep, exposed sections on the hillside traverse.

At about 7½ miles the traverse ends and the road starts a determined climb toward the top. The trail finally emerges from the trees to yield those satisfying views from the crest of the ridge (5680 feet). The road goes over the top and heads down the other side ⅛ mile, but the best views lie along the ridge crest.

Skiing the untracked slopes

52 MANASTASH RIDGE

Skill level: advanced basic
Round trip: 6 miles
Skiing time: 3 hours
Elevation gain: 1460 feet

High point: 4750 feet
Best: January–mid-March
Avalanche potential: low
Map: Green Trails, Easton

P. T. Barnum said, "There's a sucker born every minute," and those of you starting this tour may believe you are one of them after witnessing the three-ring snowmobile circus here. Take heart—we're not pulling a fast one on you. In the midst of the motorized confusion lies some excellent skiing. The logging roads in the area seem designed with skiing in mind, the clearcuts are perfect for snow play, and the open forest is neatly arranged for telemarking.

Access: Drive Highway 12 to the Highway 410 turnoff, then head north up the Naches River for 24.8 miles. Turn right on Little Naches River road No. 19. At 1.9 miles park at the base of Road 1901 (2700 feet).

Skier on Road 1901

The Tour: Start out following well-trampled Road 1901. Numerous spurs and side roads sidetrack many of the snowmobiles, so with any luck the main road will be smooth for skis. At each intersection the main road is generally obvious, wider than the rest, and always climbing. Remember, only the side roads are signed. The first intersection is passed immediately after rounding the first bend; go straight. The second intersection occurs at ½ mile (3000 feet); go left.

At 1½ miles enjoy the views of Little Bald Mountain to the southwest and Fifes Ridge rising sharply up from the American River. The sharp-eyed may even catch a brief glimpse of Mount Rainier. At 2 miles Road 1901 is joined by Road 1903. Ski to the right and continue the climb up.

At 2½ miles (3540 feet), spur road (1901)722 branches off to the right. Advanced-level skiers intent on an excellent downhill run should go right here, skiing up the spur for ½ mile to the start of jeep trail No. 676 (3840 feet). The jeep trail climbs up along a ridge for 3 miles to the summit of Manastash Ridge at 6200 feet. This steep climb requires climbing skins. With light powder snows the 2-mile ski from 5280-foot Lily Pond Lake back to the road makes a superb downhill run.

Those skiers who continue on Road 1901 will have miles of exploration in store. The road climbs from the aforementioned junction for another ½ mile, then levels out at 3750 feet for a long traverse around the South Fork Quartz Creek basin.

For a longer alternate return route, ski down Road 1903 for 1 mile, then follow abandoned spur road (1901)615 back to Road 1901 and the start. If the spur road is missed, continue down to Road 19 and ski back in the trees along the side of the road, through Kaner Flat Campground, to Road 1901.

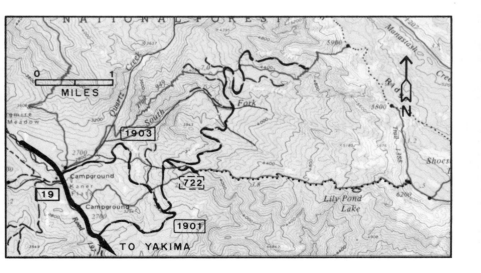

Rocky Prairie

53 ROCKY PRAIRIE

Skill level: advanced basic
Round trip: 4–18 miles
Skiing time: 3 hours–2 days
Elevation gain: 600–1617 feet
High point: 5898 feet
Best: December–April
Avalanche potential: low
Map: Green Trails, Manastash Lake

Skiing starts in late fall and lasts late into spring on the broad, rolling ridges high above the Naches River. Miles of open prairies invite exploration, and roads lead to overlooks of innumerable peaks in the South Cascades.

Access: Drive Highway 410 west from the Highway 12 junction for 13.4 miles. Turn right on Benton Creek road No. 1701 (2160 feet). Drive to the snowline and park.

The Tour: Winter trippers start at or close to the valley bottom, with 4 miles of road to ski to reach the highlands. This is snowmobile country and skiers are the oddity, so expect a few of the bolder machines to come sniffing around trying to figure out what those creatures are that move without gas tanks.

The climb starts immediately. Follow the road as it sweeps up above the Naches River with excellent views of houses and fields below. At 1½ miles stay left at a major intersection with Road 1711. The final 2½ miles to the ridge crest are in forest.

An open plain and a four-way intersection mark the arrival at Rocky Prairie (3787 feet), a good base camp for exploration. Skiers may go right 7 miles to Cleman Mountain Lookout (5115 feet), or left (north) 8 miles to Bald Mountain Lookout (5898 feet). For a little less far-flung trip, ski right ¼ mile toward Cleman Mountain, then go left 2 miles on the Rocky Prairie Road, with views to rolling hills and shimmering plains of Washington's Inland Empire.

Early and late in the season, skiers may drive all the way to Rocky Prairie, then take a left for Bald Mountain. The road climbs over a large hill to level off on Canteen Flats (4288 feet). If there is no snow here, continue north over another hill to a set of flats below Bald Mountain (5000 feet) or ski to the old Bald Mountain Lookout.

Best of all, leave roads altogether and roam for miles toward whatever tree, hill, or horizon seems intriguing.

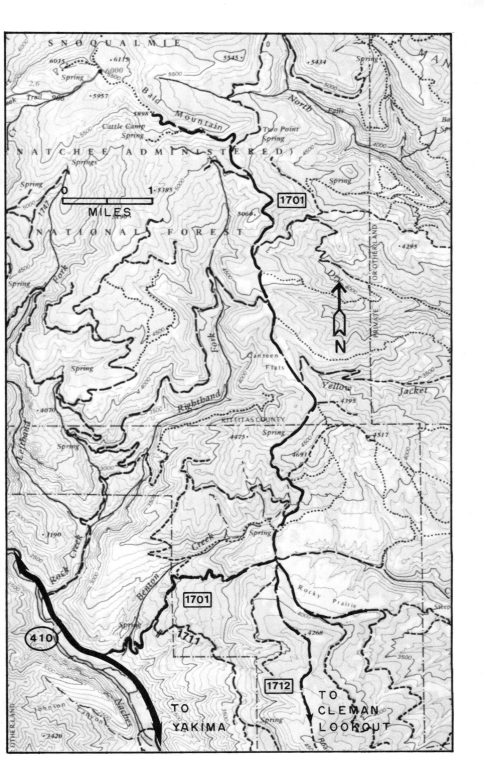

54 MOWICH LAKE

Skill level: advanced basic
Round trip: 11 miles
Skiing time: 6 hours
Elevation gain: 1410 feet
High point: 4960 feet
Best: March–April
Avalanche potential: low
Maps: Green Trails, Mount Rainier
West; USGS, Golden Lakes and
Mowich Lake

Young skier

Nestled in the forest at the base of glacier-wrapped Mount Rainier, Mowich Lake is an excellent tour for a day or weekend outing. While the area has prime skiing throughout the winter, access problems make this trip best in spring when the roads are snow-free at least to the park boundary.

Access: Drive Highway 410 to Buckley. From the west end of town turn south on Highway 165 for 10.5 miles, passing through Wilkeson and

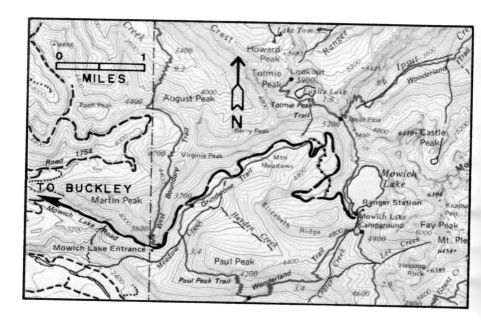

Mount Rainier from Mowich Lake Road

crossing the Fairfax Bridge over the Carbon River. At the junction beyond take the right fork to Mowich Lake. A "Road Closed" sign here indicates the road receives no winter plowing or maintenance. The pavement ends at 1.3 miles; 10 more miles on a dirt road lead to the boundary of Mount Rainier National Park (3550 feet), and the start of the tour.

The Tour: There are two ways to ski to the lake, 5½ miles on the road or by a 4½-mile road-and-trail combination suited for skiers with at least advanced-level skills. The two routes begin together on the Mowich Lake Road.

Ski through dense forest, passing the Pauls Peak Picnic Area ¾ mile from the park boundary. The road climbs gently but steadily above Meadow Creek to the end of the valley. At 3 miles (4280 feet), it makes a long curve to the south, starting the long, winding climb to the lake. Here the trail's first section leaves the road to ascend a shallow gully ¼ mile to a crossing of the road. The second section of trail stays just left of a small creek ½ mile, intersecting the road again (4640 feet). The third and final ½-mile section of trail is the steepest, rejoining the road at 4920 feet. Once back on the road (if you ever got off it), turn left and ski to its high point on the west side of Mowich Lake (4960 feet). If in doubt about the trail, stay on the road. (The Park Service may start marking the trail in years to come.)

Campsites are found at the road-end on the south side of the lake and viewpoints on the west side. For vistas from the high point of the road, ski left up a forested ridge until Mount Rainier comes in sight over the lake. Watch the thundering spring avalanches cascade down the sheer rock face of Willis Wall.

A comfortable meal after a long day of skiing

Skier's camp in Seattle Park

55 SEATTLE PARK AND RUSSELL GLACIER

*Skill level: advanced to Seattle
    Park, mountaineer to Russell
    Glacier
Round trip: 16 miles to Seattle Park
Skiing time: 2–3 days
Elevation gain: 3600 feet
High point: 6400 feet*

*Best: May–June
Avalanche potential: low
Maps: Green Trails, Mount Rainier
    West; USGS, Mowich Lake*

The north-facing slopes of Mount Rainier offer superb skiing long after the south-side snows are hard and sun-cupped. Of the numerous destinations on the north side, Seattle Park is one of the easiest to reach and provides the most rewarding views and skiing.

Above the snow-covered meadows and the clumps of trees at Seattle Park lies a telemarking paradise—two miles and over 3000 vertical feet of rolling terrain terminating at the base of Ptarmigan Ridge and the Mowich Face. The skiing is not difficult here, but the tour above Seattle Park should be reserved for skiers with mountaineering experience. Weather around Mount Rainier changes suddenly and routefinding skills are essential when the miles of nondescript slopes dissolve into a white soup.

141

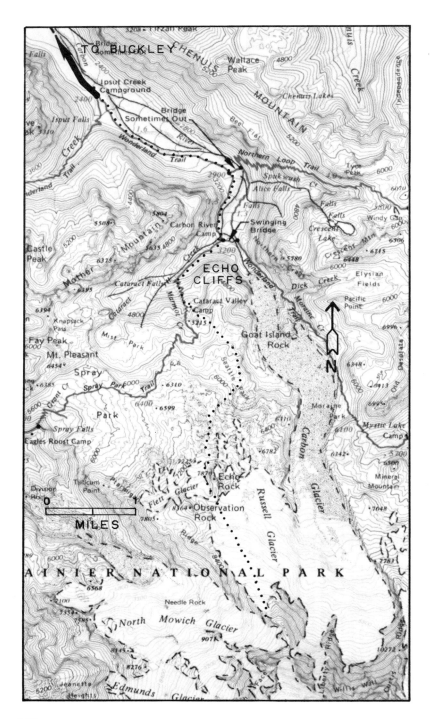

Telemarking on Russell Glacier

Access: Drive to the Carbon River Entrance of Mount Rainier National Park, register at the entrance station, then drive to the end of the road at Ipsut Creek Campground (2400 feet).

The Tour: Ski or hike up the valley on the Carbon River Trail (staying on the west side of the river for 3 miles), passing two small campsites and a trail junction. The trail crosses Cataract Creek on a log bridge to a junction at 3000 feet. Turn left on the trail if it can be found. If not, choose a course between Cataract Creek and Echo Cliffs on the hillside above. Once past Echo Cliffs (about ¾ mile up Cataract Creek, elevation 4000 feet), you'll encounter Marmot Creek. Follow it up the steep hillside to its headwaters at timberline and the base of Seattle Park.

Seattle Park extends upward for another ¾ mile, and outstanding viewpoints of Mount Rainier and Willis Wall abound. Little exploration is required to find an outstanding campsite, but it is difficult to determine which site is positively the most scenic.

Mountaineering skiers continuing up higher will discover a myriad of possibilities. Head south from Seattle Park past Echo Rock, then onto the glacier itself. There are excellent slopes on Russell Glacier all the way up to 9600 feet, before the terrain steepens. Avoid skiing too far to the east, however, where the slopes steepen, crevasses exist, and falling rocks and ice can mutilate your frail little body.

To the west and north you'll find a long succession of exhilarating ski slopes down into Spray Park. In years of low snowfall, stay off the Russell Glacier in June and ski these broad snow slopes instead.

Nisqually River valley from Stevens Canyon Road

56 REFLECTION LAKES

Skill level: intermediate
Round trip: 3 miles
Skiing time: 2 hours
Elevation gain: 538 feet
High point: 5100 feet

Best: January–mid-April
Avalanche potential: low
Maps: Green Trails, Mount Rainier
*   East; USGS, Mount Rainier East*

In summer the Reflection Lakes reflect flowers of surrounding meadows and glaciers of Mount Rainier. Most visitors pause briefly to click cameras and drive on. In winter, however, though the little snow-covered lakes reflect nothing but the sun, they are the objective of numerous day trips and overnight outings.

Access: From the Nisqually Entrance to Mount Rainier National Park follow the Paradise Road to Narada Falls Viewpoint (4572 feet). In winter a large parking area is plowed for skiers and the warming hut-restroom facility is kept open.

The Tour: From the parking lot the aim is to gain Stevens Canyon Road on the top of the steep hill straight ahead. Skiers often climb directly up the open slope behind the warming hut, but avalanche hazard rules out this approach. The safe way is to start near the warming hut and stay in the forest, climbing the left side of the open slope. The farther to the left, the easier the grade.

Once on Stevens Canyon Road, if the snow is stable, follow the road across the windswept hillside above the warming hut and another mile of

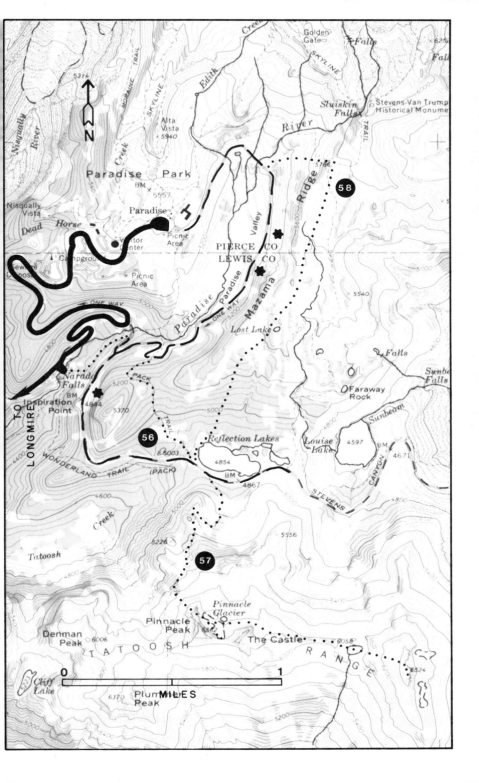

The Castle (left) and Pinnacle Peak (right) from Reflection Lakes

easy going to the lakes. The road should never be skied when conditions are unstable. If in doubt, ask a ranger before starting. If there is a possibility of avalanches, ski to the old Paradise Valley Road, follow it a short way, and pick up a ski trail, marked with orange poles, that climbs over the top of Mazama Ridge (5100 feet), then descends to Stevens Canyon Road. Ski the road ¼ mile left to the largest Reflection Lake (4861 feet).

At the lake, an obvious option is to wander the snowy meadows. Another is to visit Louise Lake. To do so, continue on the road a mile and as it begins a sharp bend to the head of Stevens Canyon leave it on the left and descend due west to the lake (4592 feet).

Other popular tours in the Lakes area are the Tatoosh Range (Tour 57) and to Paradise via Mazama Ridge (Tour 58).

MOUNT RAINIER

57 TATOOSH RANGE

Skill level: advanced
Round trip: 5 miles
Skiing time: 4 hours
Elevation gain: 1432 feet
High point: 6000 feet
Best: January–April

Avalanche potential: moderate
Maps: Green Trails, Mount Rainier
East; USGS, Mount Rainier East

Map on page 145

As viewed from a small saddle on the side of Castle Peak in the Tatoosh Range, the enormous bulk of Mount Rainier fills the entire northern horizon. Below lies a basin whose deep snow generally is much drier than that across the valley at Paradise, and the steep slopes are ideal for telemarking.

Access: From the Nisqually Entrance to Mount Rainier National Park drive to the Narada Falls Viewpoint parking area (4572 feet). Ski to Reflection Lakes (4854 feet) (Tour 56).

The Tour: Skiers who have hiked this area in the summer are familiar with the two trails from the Reflection Lakes vicinity up into the Tatoosh Range, the Bench and Snow Lakes Trail and the Pinnacle Saddle Trail. Both are highly avalanche-prone in winter. There is, however, a relatively avalanche-free entry to the Tatoosh Range via Castle Saddle.

Ski the Stevens Canyon Road halfway around Reflection Lakes. At a convenient point leave the road and start uphill into a big basin with a steep headwall. The avalanche-free route climbs the right side of the basin in the fringe of trees atop a rib. Still in trees, cross the top of the headwall and climb into another big basin between Pinnacle Peak on the right and Castle on the left. Follow the treeline on the left of the basin.

Mount Rainier from Castle Saddle

When the trees end, climb the last 200 feet of steep open slopes on the east side of Castle to the crest of the Tatoosh Range (6000 feet).

Look south to the three southern giants—the dark, steaming mass of Mount St. Helens, the sharp peak of Mount Hood, and the rounded mass of Mount Adams. All three are dwarfed by massive Mount Rainier to the north.

For most skiers the saddle is enough. However, those who wish to go farther (when the snow is stable) can cross to the south side of the saddle and head east to the next small hill, staying well away from the corniced summit. Continue to a saddle (6000 feet) below Unicorn Glacier. This is a good turnaround; beyond, the avalanche potential is high.

58 MAZAMA RIDGE

Skill level: advanced
Round trip: 6 miles
Skiing time: 4 hours
Elevation gain: 900 feet in, 900 feet
*   out*
High point: 5700 feet

Best: January–mid-May
Avalanche potential: moderate
Maps: Green Trails, Mount Rainier
*   East; USGS, Mount Rainier East*

Map on page 145

Ski the snowy meadows of Mazama Ridge with views of the ancient Tatoosh Range and the young giant of the Cascades, Mount Rainier. Then show your skill at telemarking down the steep slopes to Reflection Lakes

Skiing the open meadows of Mazama Ridge

149

and finish your tour with a long aerobic climb back up to Paradise.

The Mazama Ridge tour is fun in most weather and snow conditions and with careful navigation can even be skied in a whiteout. However, sections of the return leg of the tour on the Stevens Canyon and Paradise Valley Roads are prone to avalanche and should be skied with caution. Talk with the ranger at Paradise before starting out.

Access: Drive to the Nisqually Entrance of Mount Rainier National Park, then on to the end of the road at Paradise. The tour starts from the southeast corner of the upper parking lot (5450 feet).

The Tour: Ski the Paradise Valley Road below Paradise Inn and descend gently past the two snow-covered bridges. Directly after the second bridge (5200 feet), turn left and head uphill. If you have climbing skins, this is the time to put them on.

The climb starts out steep but levels out on a small bench. Ski to the upper end of the bench, then up the steep hill to your right. Switchback up open slopes of the crest of Mazama Ridge (5700 feet).

Take time to explore the rolling ridge crest, uninhibited by summer signs that tell you to "Stay on the Trail" and "Keep off the Meadows." Ski over a rolling cushion of snow north toward Panorama Point or to the open basin below Paradise Glacier a little to the east.

To continue the loop, head down Mazama Ridge, staying to the right of center along the ridge top. Near the southern end of the ridge, the broad plateau falls away. Ski just east of the ridge crest, angling through several open, south-facing slopes, then head down through heavy timber. Near the bottom, bear right to reach Reflection Lakes at 2½ miles (4861 feet).

To return, ski west from Reflection Lakes on Stevens Canyon Road. At ¼ mile past the lakes is the Cutoff Trail and a choice. To continue on the road means crossing a steep avalanche slope above Narada Falls, which is only safe when the snow pack is stable. If following the road, ski about halfway across the avalanche slope, then head uphill on the Paradise Valley Road. If the snow pack is unstable or you simply love the excitement of skiing steep, tree-studded hillsides, then follow the orange stakes marking the trail, up over Mazama Ridge and down to the Paradise Valley Road.

Ski up the Paradise Valley Road through the beautiful snow-covered valley with views of Mount Rainier ahead. The road traverses below Mazama Ridge, passing under an avalanche chute halfway up the valley. Here it is best to ski wide out into the open valley floor when there is any risk of avalanches.

The Castle and Pinnacle peaks from Mazama Ridge

59 CAMP MUIR

Glacier Vista

Skill level: intermediate
Round trip: 3 miles
Skiing time: 2 hours
Elevation gain: 1022 feet
High point: 6336 feet
Best: December–April
Avalanche potential: low
Maps: Green Trails, Mount Rainier
East; USGS, Mount Rainier East

Camp Muir

Skill level: mountaineer
Round trip: 9 miles
Skiing time: 8 hours
Elevation gain: 4500 feet
High point: 10,000 feet
Best: mid-October–mid-July
Avalanche potential: moderate
Maps: Green Trails, Mount Rainier
East; USGS, Mount Rainier East

Though the snow is best from mid-October to mid-July, diehards ski the year around at one place or another between Paradise and Camp Muir. Winter skiers generally are satisfied with the steep slopes at Glacier Vista below Panorama Point. Those continuing to Camp Muir should be proficient mountaineers ready to deal with sudden whiteouts and blasting winds. In summer the snowline retreats to the base of the permanent icefield above Pebble Creek (7500 feet). Even in these milder months be prepared for sudden changes of weather and fogs that erase all landmarks.

Note: When snow conditions are unstable or an east wind is blowing, causing a slab avalanche to form, Panorama Point has high avalanche po-

Horizontal ice crystals show the fury of a winter storm at Camp Muir.

tential. Stay away after a heavy snowfall, when the wind blows from the east, or during winter rains.

Access: The tour starts from the upper Paradise parking lot (5450 feet). At the start and finish of the trip register in the log book at the ranger's office.

The Tour: Ski to the left of Alta Vista, then up snowy meadows past forlorn clumps of windblown trees to Glacier Vista at 1½ miles (6336 feet). This overlook of the Nisqually Glacier is an ideal picnic spot and turnaround for winter skiers.

To proceed to Camp Muir in summer, when the snow has melted, follow the well-marked trail up the steep west face of Panorama Point. When there is snow, however, avoid the trail and climb through a broken line of dwarf trees to the right of the face on the southwest corner of the point. Skis generally are removed in favor of postholing.

Head over the rolling summit of Panorama Point, up and to the right. Ski along the left side of the prominent rock outcrops of McClure Rock and Sugar Loaf, aiming for the next knob, Anvil Rock.

Skirt it on the left and ascend the last long snowfield to Camp Muir (10,000 feet).

Ptarmigan in winter plumage

60 COPPER CREEK ROAD

Skill level: intermediate
Round trip: 14 miles
Skiing time: 7 hours
Elevation gain: 3750 feet
High point: 5600 feet
Best: mid-December—mid-April
Avalanche potential: low
Map: Green Trails, Mount Rainier West

With all the ski trails within Mount Rainier National Park, it is hard to conceive that this forest road, which crosses numerous clearcuts and is rutted by four-wheel-drive and snowmobile tracks, could be one of the most rewarding ski tours in the region. But tour it in midweek or in late spring when the snowmobilers have called it quits for the season and you're likely to agree. You'll start the tour in lowland forest among the rabbit, coyote, deer, elk, and bobcat tracks, then climb above the trees to views of Mount Adams and Mount St. Helens. The real climax of the trip, however, is the magnifying-glass view of Mount Rainier.

Access: Drive Highway 706 toward the Nisqually Entrance to Mount Rainier National Park; 5.3 miles past the town of Ashford, turn left on Copper Creek road No. 59 (1850 feet), and drive as far as possible. Trip mileages are figured from Highway 706.

The Tour: At a switchback about 2 miles up, keep left, ignoring a side road headed toward the park boundary. There are other side roads, but from here on the way is obvious. Pass by the roads that switchback to the right and the left-hand road that angles downhill.

At 4½ miles Mount St. Helens comes into view. At 5 miles Mount Adams appears on the horizon. At about 6 miles the road makes a couple of switchbacks that can be shortcut when ample snows cover the logging debris. Finally, at 7 miles reach the crest of the ridge (5600 feet), for that glorious view of Mount Rainier.

Road 59 crosses the ridge and continues north another 4 miles, but the spectacular views are lost. So if you are still energized, follow the ridge crest ½ mile east toward the steep slopes of Mount Beljica or follow the road back to the last switchback and then climb the logged-off slopes to the west for miles of ridge running.

While minimal avalanche hazard exists on Road 59, be careful on the side roads or on any steep clearcuts you decide to ski.

Mount Rainier from Copper Creek Road

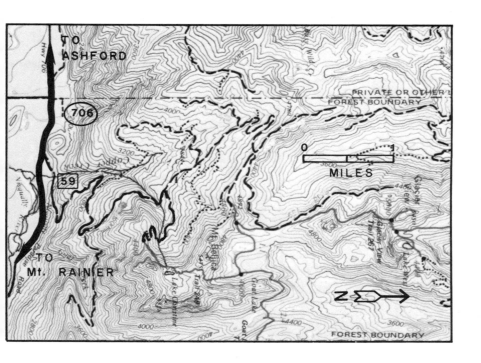

61 HIGH ROCK VIEW

Skill level: basic
Round trip: 3–20 miles
Skiing time: 2–10 hours
Elevation gain: up to 2000 feet

High point: up to 4300 feet
Best: January–March
Avalanche potential: low
Map: Green Trails, Randle

Don't classify this tour as second-rate just because it lies outside the national park boundaries. Granted, you'll receive no protection from four-wheelers or snowmobilers, but you will receive outstanding views. To the northeast rises Washington's monarch (Rainier) in her full glory and to the south lie the serrated cliffs of Sawtooth Ridge, which culminate in an obelisk-like spire known as High Rock.

View north from Road 8415

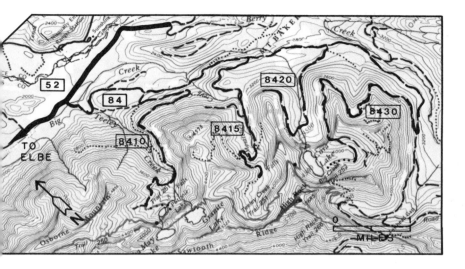

Access: Drive toward Mount Rainier National Park on State Route 706. From Ashford continue east 2.4 miles, then turn left on Forest Road 52 (Karnaham Road). After another 1.5 miles comes a 4-way intersection; go left onto Skate Creek Road (which is still Forest Road 52). Drive along the valley bottom for 3.4 miles, then take a right on Road 84 and drive to the snowline or to one of four spur roads (see below).

The Tour: The first of the four spur roads that make good ski tours starts 1.6 miles from Road 52. Road 8410 leaves Road 84 at 2320 feet and climbs for 3 miles and 1600 feet up Teeley Creek. Save this tour for the days when skiing starts at Road 52, as there are few views and frequently little snow on the lower section of the road.

The second spur road (No. 8415) starts 3 miles from Road 52 and follows Mesatchee Creek for 3 miles. The tour starts at 2700 feet with views of Nisqually Glacier, winds up through forest to views of High Rock, and ends at the edge of a clearcut (3700 feet) with views that extend all the way to the Columbian Crest.

The third tour is on spur road 8420, starting 4 miles from Road 52 (2920 feet). The gentle climb parallels Big Creek for 1½ miles to Big Creek Trail (not suitable for skiing), and ends at 2½ miles in a clearcut (3600 feet). Views along this tour are outstanding, with Mount Rainier dominating the scene and High Rock casting a long shadow over the valley.

The fourth tour starts 6.5 miles from Road 52 and is the best of the bunch. Ski up spur road 8430 starting at 3300 feet and climb around a broad hill. Views of Mount Rainier are breathtaking. Near 3½ miles the road divides; go left on spur road (8430)042 and ski ½ mile to the end of the road (3900 feet) in full view of High Rock Lookout. Advanced-level skiers may continue on with the help of a map and ski over the next hill to Cora Lake (4300 feet).

62 LOOKOUT MOUNTAIN

Skill level: advanced basic
Round trip: 7 miles to vista, 13 miles
  to mountain
Skiing time: 4 hours
Elevation gain: 2360 feet, 2995 feet

High point: 5000 feet, 5475 feet
Best: December–April
Avalanche potential: moderate
Map: Green Trails, Randle

The Lookout Mountain tour follows a logging road along Horse Creek to an open clearcut valley and snow-covered meadows. The road starts from the Nisqually River Valley (2440 feet) where the snow level fluctuates wildly throughout the winter. To accommodate the variations in the starting point, two objectives are offered. The closest is a road tour leading to a high ridge with viewpoints over the rarely seen southwest side of the Tatoosh Range, High Rock, and "The Mountain" itself. The second is a road and backcountry tour to Lookout Mountain, a forested summit that has managed to escape the ravages of the chainsaw (as of 1987).

Access: Drive toward Mount Rainier National Park on State Route 706. From Ashford continue east 2.4 miles, then turn left on Forest Road 52, Karnaham Road. At 1.5 miles turn left at a 4-way intersection (still on Road 52) and drive upriver. In 2 miles the pavement ends and at 8 miles

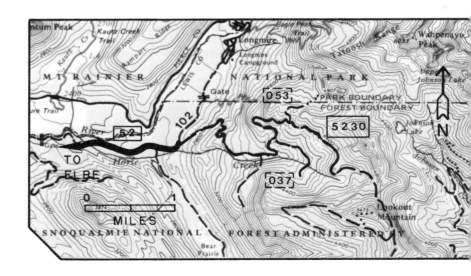

Mount Rainier from ridge below Lookout Mountain

the road divides; go left on Road 5230. Tour mileages start from this intersection (2440 feet).

The Tour: Ski or drive through heavy forest up Road 5230. At ¼ mile, spur road (5230)012 branches left toward the national park and ends at Longmire Campground. Remain on Road 5230, which begins to climb and makes one broad switchback before heading into Horse Creek Valley. At 2¼ miles, the road crosses the edge of a huge clearcut and starts another switchback.

Skiers on Lookout Mountain Road

Spur road (5230)037 is passed at 2¾ miles (3700 feet). This road winds through clearcuts and a wide basin at the head of Horse Creek, then ends at the base of a steep open slope. Skiers choosing this spur road can climb out of the basin on either the north- or south-side clearcuts to rejoin Road 5230.

Skiers who stay on Road 5230 get their first view across the valley toward Mount Rainier after 3¼ miles. The road makes a sharp bend here, climbs around Frozen Frog Pond, then heads east, contouring back across the upper reaches of Horse Creek Basin.

To reach the high ridge viewpoints, go left at 4¼ miles on spur road (5230)053 and ski steeply up to an unmarked intersection at 4½ miles. Go right, climbing first along the ridge crest, then along the side of the hill, to road's end in a clearcut. The destination is the ridge top directly above. Head up across the open slopes to reach the ridge at 5000 feet. At the top of the clearing, which is also the top of the ridge, you'll be able to look south right into the crater of Mount St. Helens. To the north rise the rocky summits of Eagle and Wahpenayo peaks and glacier-clad Mount Rainier. Ski along the ridge to find the best views through the trees of the Tatoosh Wilderness to the northwest. Use caution on the summit of the ridge, as there are several steep, body-mutilating dropoffs.

The safest way to reach Lookout Mountain is to stay on Road 5230 back at the 4¼ mile mark. At 5¼ miles the road enters a basin where a natural meadow and a clearcut create a large bowl. The road returns to forest as it climbs over a 4800-foot ridge. Skiers without backcountry experience should end their tours here.

Experienced skiers can turn left and follow the ridge to the 5475-foot summit of Lookout Mountain. The summit is partially forested, with a broad avalanche slope on the southwest side. Stick to the ridge crest. Once on top, look around for signs of the old lookout. Don't be disappointed if you can't find any—even the Forest Service no longer knows its exact location.

63 BURLEY MOUNTAIN

Skill level: intermediate
Round trip: up to 18 miles
Skiing time: 8 hours–3 days
Elevation gain: 3931 feet
High point: 5304 feet

Best: November–December and
*   March–April*
Avalanche potential: low
Map: Green Trails, McCoy Peak

From the valley Burley Mountain seems to be just one of many ridges bristling with dense second-growth forest. Those who make the long climb to the top, however, find that the miles of unrelieved timber lead to sparkling snow-covered meadows and a lookout with views which include the three southern volcanoes of Washington.

The first 7 miles of the Burley Mountain Road are mostly wooded. Most skiers therefore do the trip when it is drivable the first couple of miles. In May they are advised to check first with the Randle Ranger Station because the road may be gated in late spring to protect the winter-softened grade while it dries out.

Access: Drive to Randle. Just east of the grocery store turn off Highway 12 on the Mount Adams–Cispus Center Road heading south. When the road splits at .9 mile, stay left on the Cispus road No. 23. At 8.3 miles go right on Road 28 for 1.4 miles, then take another right on Road 76. Drive 3.3 miles, passing the Cispus Center and the small community of Tower

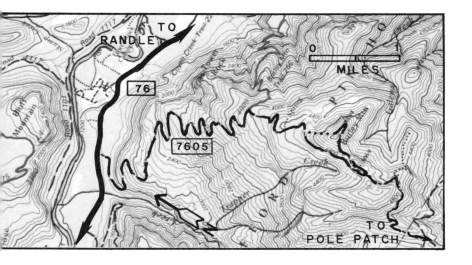

Excellent telemarking on the open slopes near the summit of Burley Mountain

Rock, to reach Burley Mountain road No. 7605. Park at the junction (1273 feet), or at the snowline.

The Tour: Burley Mountain Road starts right off climbing. Switchbacks through dense forest cover reach the first meadow at 6 miles (4260 feet), a good campsite. A short spur branches left 1000 feet to a spring (do not expect running water in winter).

The big meadows start at 7 miles as the road emerges on open slopes beneath the lookout. If snow conditions are unstable, this is the proper turnaround.

The final section of road climbs to meet a long ridge south of the lookout. The road continues 4.5 miles to Pole Patch Campground; however, Burley Mountain skiers take the left branch back to the plainly visible lookout—or climb the open meadows and cut off nearly 2 miles of road skiing.

Once at the lookout let the eye wander southwest toward the steaming remains of once-mighty Mount St. Helens, then farther east to the still-mighty Mount Adams, and finally north to the mightiest of all, Mount Rainier.

If you have an extra day just for exploring, ski south from the lookout, back along the ridge crest to the narrow forested saddle where the road crosses. Cross the road and head up into the trees to the top of the 5160-foot knoll and ski down the southwest rib side, avoiding an exposed and slide-prone section of road. Head down along the rib to the road and continue down to a saddle and a 4-way intersection (4080 feet), 2 miles from the saddle. Ski straight ahead, contouring along the east side of the ridge on well-graded road for the next 3 miles to reach the open slopes of the Pole Patch (4700 feet). You'll find excellent camping and skiing here in the huckleberry fields.

64 HAMILTON BUTTES

Cat Creek Road

Skill level: intermediate
Round trip: up to 12 miles
Skiing time: 6 hours
Elevation gain: 1800 feet
High point: 4400 feet
Best: mid-December–March
Avalanche potential: moderate
Map: Green Trails, Blue Lake

Hamilton Buttes

Skill level: advanced
Round trip: 20 miles
Skiing time: 9 hours
Elevation gain: 2878 feet
High point: 5478 feet
Best: mid-December–March
Avalanche potential: moderate
Map: Green Trails, Blue Lake

On a clear day the view of Mount Adams from the Cat Creek Road is worth a lot. It's worth putting up with buzzing snowmobiles, barking dogs pulling sleds, and even churning four-wheel-drives. So is the tour worthwhile on a cloudy day? If you're looking for miles of skiing to burn off some winter flab, the answer is yes.

Mount Rainier from the Mouse Creek road

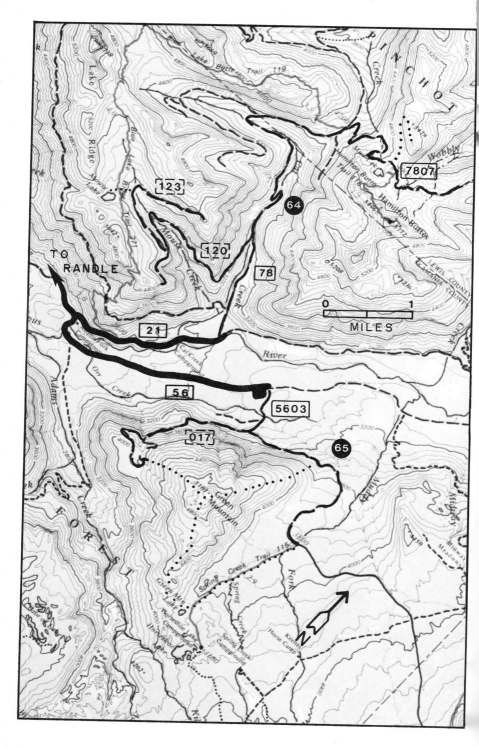

Skiers who are undaunted by the 10-mile road approach will find Hamilton Buttes an exciting destination. Their open slopes challenge skiers to scribe only their best telemarks on the inclined sheet of virgin snow. The buttes are a well-kept secret among backcountry skiers, and will probably remain the domain of a chosen few because of the long approach. Skiers who want to sap the most out of this fantastic playground should plan two days for this trip.

Access: Drive Highway 12 to Randle and follow combined Forest Roads 23 and 25 south from the center of town. In 1 mile stay left on Road 23, then drive 18 miles before taking a left on Road 21. Drive 4.7 miles to Adams Fork Campground. This is usually the end of the plowed road in winter (2600 feet). If the road is open, however, continue on Road 21 for 2 more miles to Cat Creek.

Cat Creek Road: From Adams Fork Campground, ski up Road 21 along the Cispus River. Except for a short climb right after Adams Fork, the way is mostly flat. After 1½ miles, pass Cat Creek Campground, then cross Cat Creek (2700 feet). The intersection with Cat Creek road No. 78 is found at 2 miles; ski left here. At 2¼ miles, pass up an inviting-looking side road—hazardous avalanche slopes exist along that route.
Cross Cat Creek at 3¼ miles (3100 feet), and take a left on spur road (7800)120. A steep, rapid climb rounds a shoulder and enters the Mouse Creek drainage. At 5¾ miles cross Mouse Creek, and continue ¼ mile farther to the road's end on a small logging platform where the whole Cispus River Valley unfolds below your feet east. Farther to the east sits the rounded lump of Potato Hill and to the south Green Mountain tries unsuccessfully to hide Mount Adams. If time allows, ski spur road (7800)123 for ¾ mile back around the Mouse Creek drainage. About ⅛ mile before the creek, turn uphill and climb through the trees over Blue Lake Ridge Trail to little, forested Mouse Lake (4440 feet).

Hamilton Buttes: From Adams Fork Campground ski 2 miles up Road 21, then go left on Cat Creek Road for 5 miles to a pass (4200 feet). At the far end of the pass go right on Road 7807 and switchback up the clearcut along Timonium Creek. An alternate approach is to don climbing skins at the start of the pass and climb up to reach the road.
The base of the buttes is reached at 7 miles, where the road divides. To the right, just over the hill, is little Mud Lake (4850 feet), a small patch of frozen snow surrounded by ghostly trees, remnants of the fire that swept the buttes bare.
The highest butte, site of an old lookout, is to the south, and is attainable by skiing along the west ridge. The area here is a bit cliffy for good telemarking, so if you've come to crank turns, head north from the lake to a 5478-foot butte and pick out the first of many runs from there.

65 GREEN MOUNTAIN

Viewpoint

Skill level: advanced basic
Round trip: 6 miles
Skiing time: 4 hours
Elevation gain: 1000 feet
High point: 4000 feet
Best: January–March
Avalanche potential: low
Map: Green Trails, Blue Lake

Mountain Loop

Skill level: advanced
Round trip: 8 miles
Skiing time: 6 hours
Elevation gain: 2047 feet
High point: 5107 feet
Best: January–March
Avalanche potential: low
Map: Green Trails, Blue Lake

Map on page 164

In the midst of a system of Sno-Parks on the north side of Mount Adams that seems designed for snowmobile users only, it's a bonus to find a haven where you can escape the traffic. Green Mountain is not closed to motors, but few machines venture onto this short, dead-end road while endless miles of other roads lure the beasts elsewhere.

The Green Mountain road climbs up through clearcuts to a tremendous view of Mount Adams—it's an enjoyable climb and descent for most skiers. Advanced-level skiers can reach the backcountry by continuing up from the end of the road to the summit of Green Mountain. When snow conditions are good (i.e., it isn't raining), you can make a long day of it by descending the east side of Green Mountain and returning back to the Sno-Park on Road 5603.

Access: Reaching the Sno-Park constitutes the major difficulty of this tour. After heavy snowfalls the plows may not come the long miles from Randle for several days and the parking area will be located at Adams Fork Campground. Once the spring melt is under way, the Sno-Park is located 3 miles beyond at the junction of Roads 56 and 5603.

Drive Highway 12 to Randle and at the center of town turn south on Cispus Road, also noted as Forest Roads 23 and 25. After 1 mile the road divides; stay left on Road 23 for the next 18 miles, then go left on Road 21. After 4.7 miles, go right on Road 56 to Adams Fork Campground. Park here when the snow is heavy. Conditions allowing, follow Road 56 for 3 miles to the Sno-Park at the Road 5603 turnoff and park (2960 feet).

The Tour: From the Sno-Park, follow the snowmobile tracks a few feet on Road 56 then go right on Road 5603. Ski south over the broad valley floor. Once across Orr Creek the road starts to climb to the base of Green Mountain. Turn right on Road (5603)017 at ¾ mile from the Sno-Park and leave the snowmobile route. Climb steadily to the southwest, enjoying views of Juniper and Sunrise peaks.

Mount Rainier from Green Mountain

Mount Curtis Gilbert in the Goat Rocks

At 2¾ miles round the first switchback into an open clearcut. If your destination is the viewpoint, ski 500 feet farther until the road levels and then go uphill on an old skid road to the ridge top at 3 miles (4000 feet). Ski across the old logging platform to the west and look around. On a clear day Mount Adams to the south takes on an overpowering presence, Mount Rainier to the north towers above Cat Creek, and Old Snowy and Gilbert to the east reign over the lesser summits of the Goat Rocks.

Advanced skiers with sights on the summit or the loop should stay on Road (5603)017 as it crosses a level bench, passes another clearcut, and then climbs steeply up through the forest. The road deteriorates here. Emerging into an upper clearcut, leave the road and climb straight up. Once in the trees above the clearcut the route is obvious—it follows the ridge line to the summit. You'll find this effort, which has further putrified your polypropylene, is rewarded with views even better than below.

If making a loop of this trip there are two descent routes. The shortest is the northeast ridge. Keeping to the right-hand (east) side ski down until you intercept Road 5603 at 3400 feet. Go left and ski back to the Sno-Park on road groomed for snowmobiles. The longer route from Green Mountain follows the south ridge from the summit to Green Mountain Lake, then down through the trees following the course of the Spring Creek Trail. The trail ends in a clearcut; continue north to Road 5603, then left, reaching the Sno-Park at 12 miles.

66 SNYDER MOUNTAIN LOOP

Skill level: intermediate
Round trip: 10 miles
Skiing time: 5 hours
Elevation gain: 1760 feet

High point: 4560 feet
Best: February–mid-March
Avalanche potential: moderate
Map: Green Trails, Packwood

On the Snyder Mountain Loop "view" is spelled *m-o-u-n-t-r-a-i-n-i-e-r*. The mountain dominates the northern skyline from every corner and from every vista, overshadowing all the neighboring summits. All other summits seen on this tour (such as the Tatoosh Range, Mount Adams, and the Goat Rocks) seem insignificant in comparison.

This tour strings together two logging roads to form an enjoyable loop. There are open clearings for telemarking, well-graded logging roads for fast-paced descents, and a lot of outstanding views of Mount Rainier. The ideal time to ski this tour is in late winter, when the access road is drivable for the first 4 or 5 miles.

Access: Drive Highway 12 east 13.7 miles from the Randle Forest Service Station or west 1.7 miles from the Packwood Forest Service Station. At the outskirts of Packwood turn east on Forest Road 48, opposite a power substation. Drive to the snowline. The tour description starts 5.5 miles up Road 48 at the junction with Road 4820 (2800 feet).

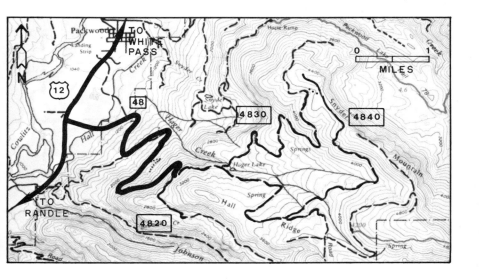

Mount Rainier from Snyder Mountain

The Tour: Ski up Road 48, enjoying the view over the city of Packwood to the Tatoosh Range and Mount Rainier. At ½ mile the road enters Hager Creek Basin and divides. Road 4830 (the left fork) is the return leg of the loop, so continue straight ahead on Road 48, watching for tracks and other signs of the elk herds that winter in this area.

The road divides again 3 miles from the start. Go left on Road 4840 and contour around Hager Creek Basin, then climb up toward the summit of Snyder Mountain. The road crests the long, rolling ridge that is called Snyder Mountain at 5 miles. Ski off the road to the right to look over into the Goat Rocks Wilderness and down to Packwood Lake before skiing the final ¼ mile to the end of the road and more outstanding views of Mount Rainier.

For the return, ski back ¼ mile from the end of the road to the point where the road crested the ridge (4480 feet). Here you head west, down the right-hand side of an open clearcut, to intersect Road 4830 (4300 feet). Go left and descend Road 4830 for 3 miles, switchbacking down the open hillside.

At 9½ miles Hager Lake is passed on the left. The road crosses Hager Creek, then climbs up to join Road 48. Go to the right and descend to your start.

67 PACKWOOD LAKE

Skill level: advanced
Round trip: 9 miles
Skiing time: 7 hours
Elevation gain: 500 feet

High point: 3200 feet
Best: January–April
Avalanche potential: low
Map: Green Trails, Packwood

An example of the difference a blanket of snow can make: Packwood Lake in summer is a turmoil of loud motorcycles and mobs trampling shores on the edge of the Goat Rocks Wilderness. In winter it is a silent island of pristine white in a sea of green peace. In summer a 4½-mile trail leads to the lake. In midwinter, if the weather so decides, there may be up to 6 additional miles of road skiing, and a party may then be well content with the trailhead parking lot's view over the Cowlitz River Valley to the Tatoosh Range and Mount Rainier. If the lake is the inflexible goal, skiers had best wait until late March or April, when the road is snow-free to the end.

Note: When the snow pack is very stable, snowmobilers and skiers bypass the trail by following the Pipeline Road ≠ Trail to the lake. At about 2 miles there is a steep side-hill section, prone to avalanches, lasting about ½ mile. If determined to try this approach, which is by far the easier, check with the Packwood Ranger Station, talk to someone who has been over the road recently, or be prepared to turn back if conditions at

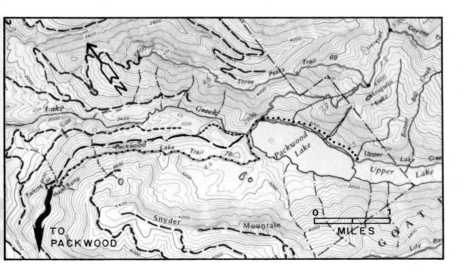

Packwood Lake Trail

the slide do not look good. The Pipeline route starts directly below the trail parking lot.

Access: Drive Highway 12 to the Packwood Ranger Station (1100 feet), and then 6 miles (if snow allows) on Packwood Lake Road to the end (2700 feet).

The Tour: Starting at the east end of the parking lot, the trail is wide, well graded, and easy to follow over gentle ups and downs. At 3½ miles a window in virgin forest looks north to Rainier. The steepest travel is the final ½ mile, where the trail drops 200 feet to the lake and campsites (2900 feet).

From here the horizon is domineered by huge walls of 7487-foot Johnson Peak. For a change of scenery ski Upper Lake Creek Trail along the east shore, to where Packwood Lake and enclosing forests form a perfect frame for the jolly white giant of the Cascades, Mount Rainier.

COWLITZ RIVER

68 YELLOW JACKET ROAD

Skill level: basic
Round trip: 7 miles
Skiing time: 4 hours
Elevation gain: 480 feet
High point: 4800 feet

Best: January–mid-April
Avalanche potential: low
Map: Green Trails, White Pass

There is fun for all in the Yellow Jacket area. The road, nearly level, pleases beginners. Clearcuts challenge intermediate and advanced skiers in search of the perfect telemark. For everyone there are maximum views for a minimum climb, especially suited to skiers seeking the best in mountain scenery but not really wanting to tackle lofty summits.

Access: Drive Highway 12 to .7 mile west of White Pass and turn north .1 mile to Yellow Jacket road No. 1284. Park well off to the side to allow road-maintenance equipment free access to the work center at the road-end (4320 feet).

The Tour: Yellow Jacket Road is a designated cross-country ski area, and consequently only a moderate number of snowmobiles get "lost" and end up here. One can follow the tracks of these poor lost souls as they wander around and around in circles.

Elevation is gained gradually along the tree-lined route. At ½ mile is the first clearcut, the best one for showing off downhill skills in linking turns. The road turns south across open slopes. Southeast, the upper lifts of the White Pass Ski Area come into view. Across the valley massive Hogback Ridge dominates the horizon. The road soon turns west and the

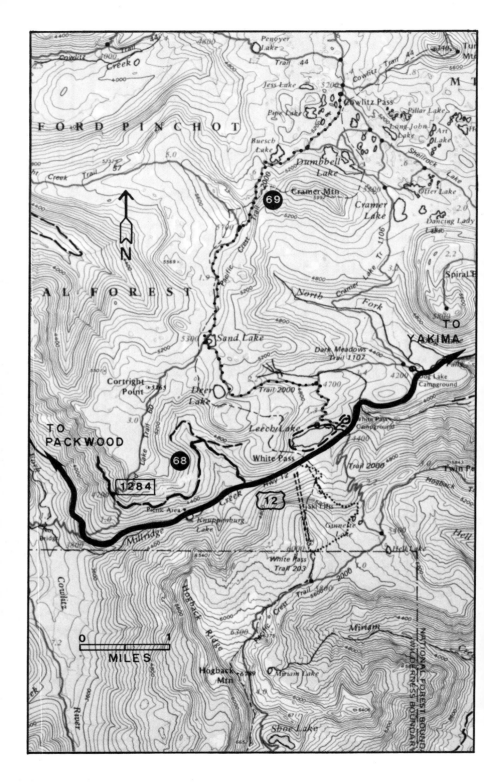

Cowlitz River Valley unfolds, a new segment being added with each clearcut traversed. On the horizon there at first is just Chimney Rock, but ultimately views extend deep into the Goat Rocks, all the way to 7930-foot Old Snowy Mountain. To the north the Tatoosh Range comes into view.

The climax of the trip is at the road-end at 3½ miles (4800 feet). When the last corner is rounded Mount Rainier emerges in full view, high and mighty above other peaks. Take a long lunch break before heading back to enjoy the miles of vistas.

Goat Rocks from Yellow Jacket Road

69 SAND LAKE

Sand Lake

Skill level: intermediate
Round trip: 7 miles
Skiing time: 6 hours
Elevation gain: 895 feet
High point: 5295 feet
Best: January–mid-May
Avalanche potential: none
Map: Green Trails, White Pass

Map on page 174

Cowlitz Pass

Skill level: advanced
Round trip: 16 miles
Skiing time: 2–3 days
Elevation gain: 1200 feet in,
  500 feet out
High point: 5600 feet
Best: January–May
Avalanche potential: low
Map: Green Trails, White Pass

Ski to one subalpine lake or to a hundred. Climb to the top of one or many of the countless hills for the sheer pleasure of coming down, or save energy and dignity by contouring. No matter what kind of cross-country is your cup of tea, the Pacific Crest Trail north of White Pass probably has it. Skiers with only one day may travel to Deer and Sand lakes. Those with two or more days can continue to the center of the lakes area at Cowlitz Pass, a wonderful base camp for explorations.

Access: Drive Highway 12 east of White Pass summit .5 mile and park at the far end of the downhill ski area parking lot (4400 feet).

The Tour: Ski through a narrow band of trees to a prepared cross-country track around Leech Lake. Turn right on the track to the northeast end of the lake and the Pacific Crest Trail.

The trail starts off in forest, switchbacking up a small knoll; the way is usually well tracked and easy to follow as far as Deer Lake. After a new snowfall, however, someone has to be first and it may be you, so be sure to carry a map and compass to navigate over the forested ridges. A brief description: After leaving Leech Lake, when nearing the top of the first hill, head left over a shallow saddle, then contour left around the backside of the open hill above Leech Lake. At 2 miles pass a large meadow on the right. Continue climbing to the left (west) up a steep ridge. A short descent down the opposite side leads to Deer Lake (5206 feet).

Beyond Deer Lake the trail turns north (right). Head along a broad ridge crest of open forest interspersed with pocket-size meadows. Sand Lake (5295 feet) lies ½ mile beyond Deer Lake and is much more difficult to spot—its odd shape makes it look more like a meadow than a body of frozen water. Day skiers should turn around at Sand Lake or whenever they've had enough exploring.

Skiing the Pacific Crest Trail south of Sand Lake

The route beyond is a steady climb along the east side of the ridge in view of Spiral Butte (an infant volcano) with occasional looks south to the Goat Rocks and Mount Adams. At 5 miles (5600 feet), the trail bends right to contour the east side of a partially forested hill, starting a descent that ends 1 mile later at Buesch Lake (5080 feet). The trail skirts the right side of the lake, then climbs northeast to Cowlitz Pass (5200 feet) and camping.

Numerous tours can be made from a base camp here. Advanced skiers enjoy the ascent of 6340-foot Tumac Mountain (another potential St. Helens) to excellent views. Intermediate skiers find plenty of room for exploration among the lakes or in Blankenship Meadows on the north side of Tumac.

Continuing north on the Pacific Crest Trail from the lakes looks inviting on the map, but avalanche potential increases dramatically.

TIETON RIVER

70 ROUND MOUNTAIN

Road's End

Skill level: advanced basic
Round trip: 9 miles
Skiing time: 5 hours
Elevation gain: 1280 feet
High point: 4320 feet
Best: January–March
Avalanche potential: low
Map: Green Trails, White Pass

Summit Tour

Skill level: mountaineer
Round trip: 9 miles
Skiing time: 6 hours
Elevation gain: 2931 feet
High point: 5971 feet
Best: January–March
Avalanche potential: high
Map: Green Trails, White Pass

Although primarily a road that tunnels through dense forest, the Round Mountain Road occasionally yields beautiful, head-on views of the Goat Rocks, where Old Snowy, Ives Peak, and Gilbert Peak dominate the skyline cloaked in their winter whites. From road's end, backcountry skiers—capable of reading a map for direction and the slopes for avalanche hazard—will find easy access to a north-facing bowl just below the summit of Round Mountain. It's a great slope for cranking turns and a superb location for burning film.

Access: Turn south off Highway 12 at 26.2 miles west of the Highway 410 junction or 7.6 miles east of White Pass. Follow the Tieton River Road 3.3 miles to the skiers' Sno-Park (3040 feet). Walk or ski ¼ mile back to the Round Mountain road No. (1200)830.

The Tour: The road climbs steadily for ½ mile, passing Road (1200)831, making a switchback, then leveling off at a viewpoint of the Goat Rocks.

Deep powder on the upper slopes of Round Mountain

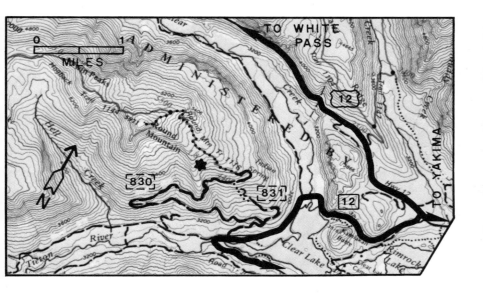

Visually this is the high point of the tour, although more views of the Goat Rocks, Clear Lake, Pinegrass Ridge, and Russell Ridge await you. For the next 3½ miles, the road alternates between lackadaisical climbing and level traversing. The road ends at the Round Mountain trailhead (4320 feet).

Skiers making the summit push may shortcut Road (1200)830 by skiing up Road (1200)831, which branches off about ½ mile from the beginning and provides a more straightforward approach to the top. Ski to road's end, then don climbing skins and head through the trees to a logged-over area on the right. Ski up to rejoin Road (1200)830 and stay with it to its end at the Round Mountain trailhead.

Now head up the mountain, sticking to the ridge crest until reaching the edge of the trees at about 5100 feet. This is the only area of potential avalanche hazard. If the snow is unstable, turn around and enjoy the tree skiing. If stable conditions allow, traverse left and climb to the summit ridge. Follow this ridge southwest to the old lookout site (5971 feet). Before returning, ski off the north side and scribble a signature or two in that tantalizing powder bowl.

TIETON RIVER

71 LOST LAKE

Skill level: advanced basic
Round trip: 10 miles
Skiing time: 6 hours–2 days
Elevation gain: 1200 feet

High point: 3800 feet
Best: January–March
Avalanche potential: none
Map: Green Trails, Rimrock

Have no fear, Lost Lake is lost no more. In summer a paved road winds up from the valley floor to a small campground at this lake nestled below the fortresslike summits of Divide Ridge. In winter the road becomes a snow-covered avenue through parklike forests of ponderosa pine. A camp at Lost Lake is ideally situated for exploring the many roads and trails that crisscross the area's meadows and lakes. Do carry map and compass here, in case *you* get lost among the maze of clearcuts and meadows.

Access: Drive 16.4 miles east of White Pass on Highway 12 (or .6 mile west of Hause Creek Campground). Turn south on Tieton Road and drive .2 mile to a large Sno-Park on the right (2550 feet). Here a large Forest Service information sign marks the start of the Goose Egg Trail, a fun 4-mile ski through the forest for novices. If there is ample snow to ski, park here. If not, turn left on Lost Lake road No. 1201 and continue driving to the snowline.

180

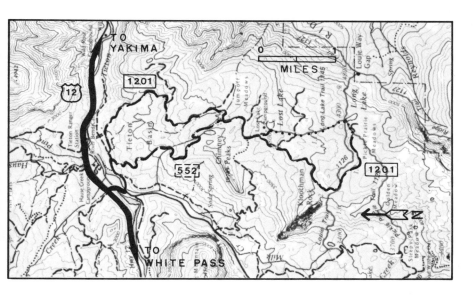

Lost Lake and Divide Ridge

Lost Lake Road

The Tour: Elevation is gradually gained on the first mile of the Lost Lake road. Several spur roads are passed—three on the right and two on the left—then the uphill grade increases slightly. Few views adorn the road here but the white snow, green pine needles, orange-red bark of the ponderosa, and blue sky more than compensate. After 2½ miles, snow-plastered Bethel Ridge to the north highlights the surroundings. At 4¾ miles, short spur road (1201)562 goes left to Lost Lake and the campground (3800 feet).

Those of you who would like to get thrown for a loop can now ski the Long Lake Trail No. 1145 from the west end of Lost Lake. The mile-long trail winds through forest, crosses logging roads, and cuts through clearcuts. Because the trail is rarely visible under a heavy blanket of snow, expect to navigate with your map and compass.

At Long Lake ski right (west), past a small shelter, and follow the road out to a large parking lot. Turn left here and ski ⅛ mile to Road 1201. (Pickle Prairie Meadows off to the left offer more fine skiing.) To close the loop, ski to the right, down Road 1201 for 3 miles back to the Lost Lake turnoff.

For a looping return to the start, at ¾ mile below Lost Lake go left on Road (1201)552. You'll rejoin Road 1201 just ½ mile from the Sno-Park.

72 BEAR CANYON

Skill level: intermediate
Round trip: 10 miles
Skiing time: 4 hours
Elevation gain: 2200 feet

High point: 4200 feet
Best: January–February
Avalanche potential: high
Map: Green Trails, Tieton

Visit Bear Canyon to explore—not to speed through. This narrow cleft twisting through the steep hillsides is characterized by beautiful red cliffs of columnar basalt. Some of the cliffs lie tinseled with giant icicles while the surrounding trees are flaked with snow. And usually the tracks of coyote and elk weave irregular patterns across the white blanket over which you ski.

A word of warning about skiing this scenic, narrow canyon: avoid it on very warm days, during or after heavy snowfall, or during unseasonal rains. At such times high avalanche danger exists.

Access: Drive Highway 12 east from White Pass 20.5 miles or west from the Highway 410 turnoff for 4.7 miles, and turn north onto Bear Canyon Road and park (2000 feet).

The Tour: Start with an easy ski across the open flood plains of the Tieton River Valley. Follow the road to a narrow cliff in the solid line of

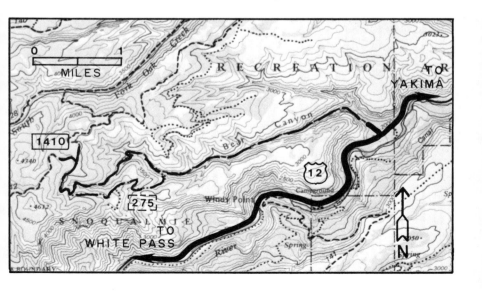

the valley walls and skim below the base of a tall wall of columnar basalt. Once under the cliffs, Bear Canyon Road temporarily ends. The valley narrows here and Bear Creek frequently floods the entire area. Ski left of the road and, for the next ¼ mile, cross and recross the creek several times following the path of least resistance up the valley. Bear with it; the washout eliminates four-wheel-drives and snowmobiles at this end of the valley.

Beyond the washout, follow a section of road littered with boulders. Thread through these obstacles and some brush until the road and valley open up to longer stretches of free skiing.

At 3 miles, after crossing Bear Creek some 14 times, come to a side road, No. (1301)275, that takes off to the left. If you feel like leaving the valley floor for a view, ski up this steep spur road to the first corner and a delightful lunch spot. Spur Road (1301)275 may be followed up and over a 4000-foot hill to rejoin the Bear Canyon Road in 1½ miles.

Continuing up the valley on Bear Canyon Road, you'll notice increasing evidence of the snowmobiles which reach this area from Oak Creek. The road begins to climb, giving the promise of a delightful descent and views of the endless procession of snow-covered hills confining the valley.

At 4½ miles Road (1301)275 rejoins the Bear Canyon Road (3800 feet). The road then makes a quick switchback marking the final push out of the canyon to the ridge top. Now a short descent leads to the upper end of Road 1410 from the South Fork Oak Creek (4000 feet). Up here the world is spread out before your skis. Glistening meadows and open forest beckon you to explore farther—just remember it gets dark early in the canyon, so allow plenty of time for the return trip.

Frozen waterfall in Bear Canyon

73 THE ELK TOUR

Skill level: intermediate
Round trip: 4 miles or more
Skiing time: 2 hours or more
Elevation gain: 1100 feet or more
High point: 3600 feet and up

Best: January–February
Avalanche potential: low
Maps: USGS and Green Trails,
Tieton and Manastash Lake

It's like being on safari. You'll see the hoofprints, the tufts of hair, and the ever-present droppings. You'll also see the mighty elk themselves, so come armed with a camera, and the trophies from your safari may be some beautiful pictures for your wall. Best of all, this is one safari where you look at the animals without glancing over your shoulder, wondering if a big cat is licking its chops while looking at you.

This tour visits the Oak Creek Wildlife Area, an elk feeding station set up to keep hungry animals out of the farms and orchards down the valley *and* to keep them out of the farmers' stewpots. The elk are fed daily at specific locations and the public is welcome to watch. January is the best time to see the animals; winter is at its peak and the elk rely on the feeding for survival. By February, portions of the herd have wandered away to fend for themselves and skiers will find elk trails winding up and over the mountains.

Access: Drive west 1.2 miles from the Highway 410 junction along Highway 12 (or east 32.6 miles from White Pass). Oak Creek Road is lo-

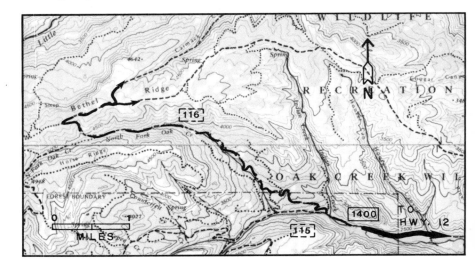

Elk sparring near the feeding area

cated on the north side of Highway 12 and is open to the public from 9 A.M. to 4 P.M. Try to arrive by 9 A.M. to watch the elk feeding, 3 miles from the highway. Skiing starts 4 miles from the main highway (2500 feet).

The Tour: Frankly, the first section of the tour is unpleasant. You start out on a road shared with a crew of snowmobiles, four-wheel-drives, and cars that think they're four-wheel-drives. This lasts for ½ mile to the first intersection. Go uphill on Road (1400)115, signed "North Fork Oak Creek," and in 200 feet take a left at a second intersection onto Road (1400)116, leaving behind all but the skiers and the snowmobiles.

Climb steadily through forest and past several open areas, paralleling the elk pathways. You'll probably see lots of coyote tracks following the elk's. At 1½ miles (3100 feet) comes an opportunity to leave behind the snowmobiles. There's no mistaking this intersection, as it's the first one in a mile. This road climbs to the right, heading steeply up for ½ mile, then dies out at 3600 feet.

Skiers choosing to ski farther should stay with Road (1400)116 and climb along the North Fork of Oak Creek. The road splits at 5 miles; the left fork stays with the creek and the right fork climbs up to join the Bethel Ridge Road at 5¾ miles.

No matter how great the snow or how blue the sky, don't forget that the gate is locked at 4 P.M.

74 MOUNT WASHINGTON

Skill level: intermediate
Round trip: up to 14 miles
Skiing time: 3–6 hours
Elevation gain: 2700 feet

High point: 3600 feet
Best: January–March
Avalanche potential: moderate
Map: Green Trails, The Brothers

On a sunny day the scenery can't be beat. Ski Big Creek Road for miles as it wanders along slopes of 5944-foot Mount Ellinor and its next-door neighbor, 6255-foot Mount Washington. Gaze out over Hood Canal and Puget Sound to Mount Rainier.

Access: From Hoodsport on Highway 101 drive Lake Cushman Road 9 miles to the end of pavement; go right 1.5 miles on Road 24, then left on Big Creek Road No. 2419 to the snowline—wherever that may be as dictated by the mood of the season and the mood of the day.

The Tour: Since a party won't know in advance how far it can drive, the trip plan must be flexible. Road 2419 starts at an elevation of 900 feet and goes nearly 7 miles to end in a clearcut at 3510 feet. It may therefore be a 14-mile day—or much less, depending.

The road sets out from 900 feet in a steady climb for the first 2½ miles, the angle easing off as a spur road is passed. Big Creek is crossed at 3 miles and a long traverse begins along the side of Mount Washington. At 3½ miles a short spur leads to a clearcut with a broad vista over Lake Cushman and Prospect Ridge. At 3¾ miles pass the Mount Ellinor Trail-

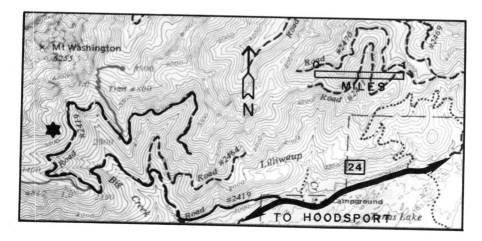

Mount Washington from Big Creek Road

head (3500 feet); the lower stretch of this trail is wooded, narrow, and steep, and the upper portion has avalanche hazard, so skiing is not recommended.

At 4½ miles the road splits. The left fork goes to a clearcut with views down on Lake Cushman; in midwinter, or when snow is unstable, this is a good turnaround-picnic spot (3600 feet).

For broader views of Puget Sound waterways and cities and Cascade peaks take the right fork (straight ahead), which gains very little elevation as it traverses beneath steep—and avalanche-prone—slopes of Mount Washington to the Mount Washington Trailhead, another route not recommended for skiing. The road bears eastward along a ridge, rounds a corner, heads north, and at 7 miles ends in a clearcut (3510 feet).

Mount Lincoln (on the right) from Four Stream Road

75 FOUR STREAM ROAD

Skill level: advanced basic
Round trip: up to 9 miles
Skiing time: up to 5 hours
Elevation gain: up to 1800 feet
High point: 3000 feet

Best: January–March
Avalanche potential: low
Maps: Green Trails, Mount Steel
and Mount Tebo

Ski from the shores of Lake Cushman up through virgin-timber national park and clearcut national forest to a view of the southern Olympics rarely seen except by loggers.

Access: From Hoodsport on Highway 101 drive Lake Cushman Road 9 miles to the end of pavement. Turn left along the lakeshore on Road 24 and follow it 5 miles, to near the head of the lake. Go left on Four Stream road No. 2451, which quickly crosses the North Fork Skokomish River, the base point of this trip (800 feet). Continue driving Road 2451 to the snowline, which is a mile or two from the river except in periods of unusually deep snow.

The Tour: Four Stream Road climbs steeply and narrowly from the valley floor, blasted from the rocky hillside. At 1½ miles enter Olympic National Park and at 2½ miles leave it at the beginning of a succession of clearcuts. Cross Elk Creek beneath a cliffy shoulder of Lightning Peak. Look northeast to 6154-foot Mount Pershing, 6255-foot Mount Washington, Mount Ellinor, and Copper Mountain.

At 4 miles the road splits. The right fork wanders on for miles through Four Stream drainage. Ski left for the big views. In a scant ½ mile go left to the ridge top and get out the lunch.

Up the North Fork Skokomish, count the valleys on the west side; the valley below you is Four Stream, the next is Five Stream, then Six, Seven, Eight, and Nine, all about a mile apart. North and east are the rugged summits of Mount Lincoln and Copper Mountain, wearing their white winter overcoats. South is Lightning Peak, its imposing cliffs making it seem much higher than 4654 feet.

Before returning, try a few downhill runs in the clearcuts.

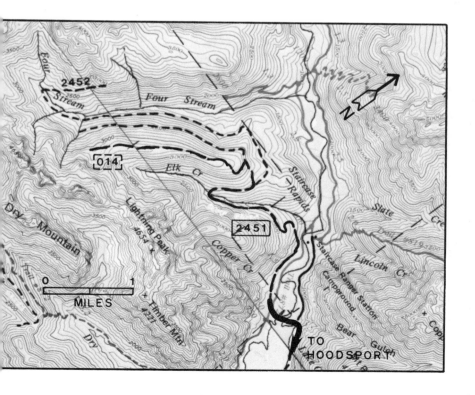

76 MOUNT TOWNSEND

Viewpoint

Skill level: basic
Round trip: 7 miles
Skiing time: 4 hours
Elevation gain: 600 feet
High point: 3900 feet
Best: January–March
Avalanche potential: low
Map: USGS, Tyler Peak

Summit

Skill level: mountaineer
Round trip: 8 miles
Skiing time: 10 hours
Elevation gain: 3175 feet
High point: 6200 feet
Best: April–May
Avalanche potential: high
Map: USGS, Tyler Peak

Steep rugged terrain and gated roads combine to make winter access to high country of the Olympics nearly impossible. However, at the northern end of the range is one outstanding exception, where open logging

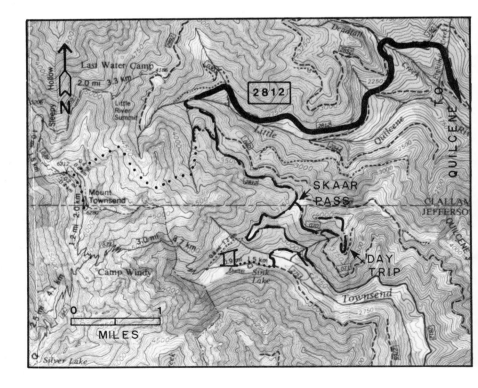

When snow blocks the road you may have to do some hiking. Mount Townsend in distance

roads pass below the white ramparts of Mount Townsend to overlooks of Puget Sound and volcanoes of the Cascades. Trip possibilities are numerous, ranging from half-day tours to overlooks, a full day or backpack to a little lake, and the very challenging and strenuous ascent of Townsend itself.

Access: Drive Highway 101 north from Quilcene 1.5 miles. Turn left on Lords Lake Road for 2.9 miles. Just before the lake, turn left on Road 2909 for 3.6 miles to a major intersection. Take the extreme left fork and head downhill on Road 2812. In .5 mile is another junction; stay on Road 2812 as it turns right, heading up the Little Quilcene River Valley towards Mount Townsend. The tour starts at the Little Quilcene River bridge (3025 feet). (After heavy snowfalls be prepared to start skiing sooner—perhaps from Highway 101.)

The Tour: Cross the bridge and ski 2 miles along clearcut slopes in an ever-growing panorama of the Cascades from Glacier Peak to Mount Baker. At Skaar Pass (3700 feet), Mount Rainier is added to the row of giants.

View seekers should take the left spur on the south side of the pass and ski 1 mile, traversing east and then climbing to the summit of a knoll, 3900 feet, for an overlook of Hood Canal and island-dotted Puget Sound.

For longer trips descend from Skaar Pass 1000 feet in 3 miles to Townsend Creek. Follow the Mount Townsend Trail ½ mile, gaining 150 feet to a small three-sided shelter in the flats of Sink Lake (2950 feet).

Topnotch skiers may wish to challenge the steep slopes and bowls of

Mount Townsend. At ½ mile past the bridge over the Little Quilcene River turn uphill on an overgrown spur road. Ski around a forested ridge and ascend a clearcut to the top (4000 feet). Just to the left of the old spar-pole landing follow a small creek into dense timber. After 100 yards cross to the right side of the creek and head for a small notch (4700 feet). On the other side is the first of several basins. Ski northwest into a large forested bowl and good camping. Traverse the bowl and climb a narrow chute that slices through a 200-foot band of rock cliffs. Then follow lightly timbered slopes up to open meadows and the long ridge leading to the summit (6200 feet).

77 OBSTRUCTION POINT

Waterhole Camp
Skill level: intermediate
Round trip: 7 miles
Skiing time: 5 hours
Elevation gain: 200 feet
High point: 5000 feet
Best: January–April
Avalanche potential: low
Map: Green Trails, Mount Angeles

Obstruction Point
Skill level: advanced
Round trip: 16 miles
Skiing time: 2 days
Elevation gain: 1300 feet
High point: 6200 feet
Best: January–April
Avalanche potential: low
Map: Green Trails, Mount Angeles

The Olympic Mountains have been the victim of bad press in the cross-country world, where stories abound of terrific winter storms and steep terrain. However, a day on Hurricane Ridge, the range's most popular ski area, can put those stories out of mind. The Obstruction Point Trail avoids the crowds of Hurricane Hill (Tour 78) and leads to excellent skiing in winter beauty and solitude. Day-trippers can enjoy a tour to Waterhole Camp; overnighters can make the panoramic beauty of Obstruction Point their goal.

Access: From Port Angeles drive 17 miles to Hurricane Ridge. Before setting out, register your tour at the Visitor Center. Day skiers can park at the road-end. Overnighters, after registering, must drive back down the road 2½ miles to a parking area, lest their cars be buried by drifting snow in the exposed upper lot.

The Tour: The Obstruction Point Trail begins, well marked, ½ mile before the day lodge at the last major turn in the highway (4900 feet). Day-trippers can ski part of the way down from the upper lot to the trailhead, but the last ¼ mile is on a steep slope and it's best to walk the road. Overnighters, obviously, will drop all packs and most of the party at the

194

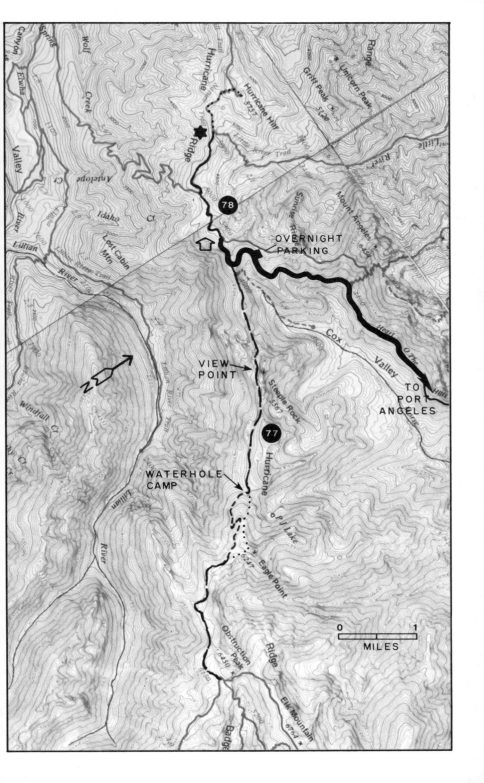

Steeple Rock and Eagle Point from Hurricane Ridge

trailhead; the driver either can hitch a ride up from the lower lot, usually no problem, or ski the roadside.

In the first ¼ mile the trail drops sharply to the Obstruction Point (summer) road. It then traverses rolling, forested terrain, breaking into the open at 1½ miles on the south side of Steeple Rock. Views extend over the Bailey Range and the Alaskan-looking, 7965-foot lord of the area, Mount Olympus. In icy snow or bad weather make the edge of the clearing the turnaround.

Beyond the clearing the way reenters forest, traverses two more small hills, and at 3½ miles reaches Waterhole Camp (5000 feet), a good turnaround for day skiers—keep in mind that the road is gated at dusk.

Overnighters continuing to Obstruction Point face a 900-foot climb in the next ½ mile, passing 6247-foot Eagle Point on its south side. The last 3 miles to Obstruction Point traverse open meadows above the treeline, exposing skiers to grand views, sometimes dangerously icy hills, and perhaps bad weather. The final mile climbs to the end of Obstruction Point Road (6150 feet), with excellent views and campsites. Travel beyond the point is not recommended due to high avalanche potential.

78 HURRICANE HILL

Ridge Road

Skill level: intermediate
Round trip: 3 miles
Skiing time: 2 hours
Elevation gain: 200 feet
High point: 5200 feet
Best: January–mid-April
Avalanche potential: none
Map: Green Trails, Mount Olympus

Hilltop

Skill level: advanced
Round trip: 6 miles
Skiing time: 4 hours
Elevation gain: 760 feet
High point: 5757 feet
Best: January–mid-April
Avalanche potential: moderate
Map: Green Trails, Mount Olympus

Map on page 195

Don't expect to be alone on wide-open, gleaming slopes amid the scenery that in 1982 led the United Nations to designate Olympic National Park a World Heritage Park. In good weather throngs of nordic skiers swarm the unplowed road from Hurricane Ridge Visitor Center along the rolling ridge toward Hurricane Hill. "Hurricane" is a deserved name and often the road is deeply scooped by wind cirques, so most skiers are content with views over the Elwha River and the Bailey Range from the halfway point.

Access: From Port Angeles drive 17 miles to Hurricane Ridge. Register your trip destination at the Visitor Center (5200 feet).

Mount Olympus (center) from Hurricane Hill

Snow-plastered trees at the summit of Hurricane Hill

The Tour: Ski west from the lodge, skirting the downhill ski area and passing through the snow-play area; watch out for flying inner tubes and their screaming pilots who are having the times of their lives. The route follows a summertime road along the ridge, descending the first mile, then leveling and climbing a bit to the picnic area at 1½ miles.

A skiers' information board marks the start of the second half, the 1½ miles beyond the road-end to Hurricane Hill. Beyond here, competence in telemark and/or kick-turn is essential. So is an eye for the weather, which in an hour can change from balmy sunshine to blinding blizzards. Be prepared for a quick retreat.

Part of the way is on a very narrow ridge which windblown snow gives a knife-edge crest. Stay atop the ridge and climb over a small knoll rather than trying to traverse its very steep and dangerous sides; in unstable or icy conditions this is mandatory. Ski down the far side of the knoll, wary of cornices on the north (right), then around a second knoll to the foot of Hurricane Hill.

A rock outcrop amid stunted, wind-blasted trees marks the summit (5757 feet). Gaze over Port Angeles, the Strait of Juan de Fuca, Victoria, Vancouver Island mountains, the British Columbia Coast Range, and, of course, Mount Baker. Reach for another sandwich and turn to gaze over Olympus and the Elwha Valley.

On the way back from the picnic area save time to explore open slopes south of the ridge road.

79 MOUNT ADAMS

Skill level: mountaineer
Round trip: 8 miles
Skiing time: 10 hours
Elevation gain: 6000 feet
High point: 12,276 feet
Best: May–mid-July

Avalanche potential: low
Maps: Green Trails, Mount Adams
West; USGS, Mount Adams East

We all have favorite ski tours—ones we can't find enough superlatives to describe—and in our opinion the tour up the long southern ridge of Mount Adams qualifies as one of the finest trips in Washington.

The trek up the state's second highest peak roughly follows the old mule trail to the summit and is entirely crevasse-free. Views of the surrounding volcanoes—Hood, St. Helens, Rainier—reward your toil, but the real prize is the descent. Imagine a 6000-foot vertical drop down a 4-mile ridge and you'll understand why people come back year after year.

Although the skiing is not difficult, this tour is extremely demanding. Skiers must carry the survival gear necessary for climbing any major peak. Prepare yourself for sudden changes in the weather; carry wands and a compass to aid in the descent should clouds quickly engulf the summit, as they are known to do.

The long south-facing slope is often ready for skiing before the access roads are snow-free. Call the ranger station at Trout Lake for road conditions before establishing a date to ski the mountain. In May, plan on an overnight tour that could include up to 7½ miles of road skiing to reach Timberline Camp. In mid-July plan on having to walk as much as a mile from the end of the road to reach snow.

Access: Early-season access to Mount Adams is via the Columbia River Highway 14 and State Route 141 to Trout Lake, where climbers and skiers must register. Then head 1.4 miles north of Trout Lake on Highway 141. Turn right on a road signed "Mount Adams Recreation Area" and drive .6 mile before turning left on Road 80. Follow signs to Morrison Creek Campground, then on to Timberline Camp at road's end (6000 feet). Road numbers change during the drive from 80 to 8040 then to Spur 500.

Later in the season skiers coming from the north can save considerable time by driving Forest Road 23 south from Randle to Trout Lake.

The Tour: Leave Timberline Camp from the west side of the climbers' parking area, following a low ridge north and slightly east. Angle around the west side of South Butte to the base of Suksdorf Ridge (7600 feet). Using the right side of the ridge as a guide, follow the ridge to the false summit (11,657 feet).

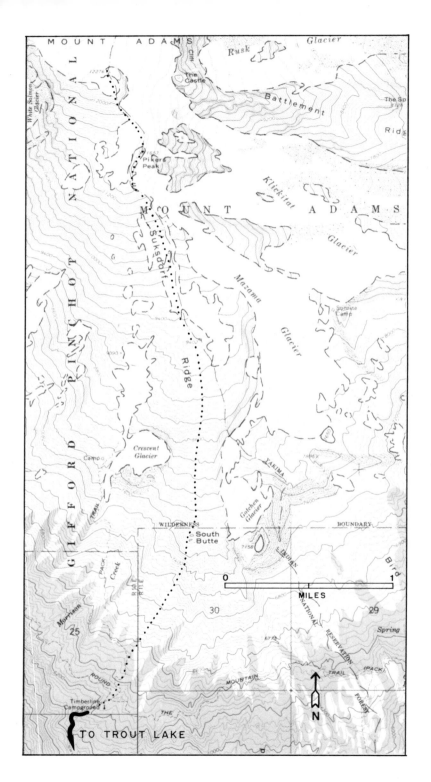

TO TROUT LAKE

The old lookout at the summit of Mount Adams is visible in the late summer only.

Ski over the level crater then up the final, rather steep 600 feet to the true summit (12,276 feet). Weather and time permitting, plan a long rest at the summit—your thighs are going to need help to survive that long run down. On clear days look down on Mount Jefferson, Mount Hood, Goat Rocks, and Mount St. Helens. Then turn north and look up to Mount Rainier—the only point in Washington State that stands over you.

On the descent, stay close to your ascent route. Avoid the tendency to drift east onto the open and crevassed slopes of the Mazama Glacier or west into avalanche-prone gullies.

80 APE CAVE TOUR

Skill level: basic
Round trip: 5 miles
Skiing time: 4 hours
Elevation gain: 1000 feet
High point: 2800 feet

Best: January–February
Avalanche potential: none
Map: Green Trails, Mount St.
  Helens

Despite spectacular views of Mount St. Helens, miles of road to explore, and an annual winter closure to motorized use, the chief attraction of this tour is the Ape Cave. So even if you have the intention of spending the entire day on your skis, be sure to pack a good flashlight and a set of spare batteries just in case one of your party members has never had the opportunity to explore a lava tube.

Access: Take the Woodland exit off Interstate 5 and head east on Highway 503 for 28.8 miles to the town of Cougar. Drive east, past Cougar, for 6.8 miles, then go left on Forest Road 83 for 1.7 miles. Turn left on Forest Road 8303 for the final .2 mile to the parking area, picnic area, and gate (1800 feet).

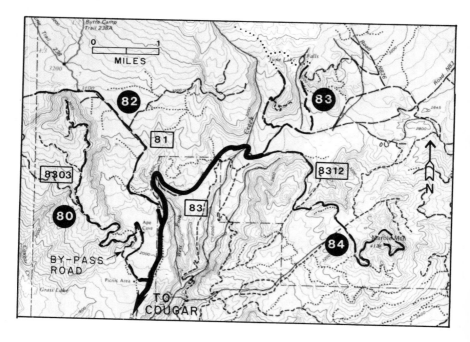

Entrance to the Ape Cave

The Tour: Before putting the skis on, limber up by exploring around the picnic area. Besides such obvious attractions as outhouses and picnic tables, there is a nature trail around a small section of ground riddled with lava casts of long-gone trees.

The tour follows Road 8303, starting from the gate. Enjoy the level ground while it lasts, then prepare for a stiff climb. The road divides at ½ mile; beginners and cave explorers should stay to the right. (The left fork is a cave bypass route which rejoins the cave road 1 mile beyond. The bypass road is very steep in sections.)

The Ape Cave parking lot is reached near 1 mile and the cave entrance a couple of hundred feet beyond (2070 feet). The majority of skiers and hikers stop at the cave and never continue, so the following is a description of what you will miss if you stop here.

Past the cave the road levels for ⅛ mile, then begins climbing again. At 1½ miles the cave bypass road joins on the left and the combined roads continue an easy climb. At 2 miles the road climbs onto a broad, rolling ridge crest. In the meadowlike openings there are views northeast to Mount St. Helens and excellent picnic spots.

Near 2½ miles the road divides (2800 feet). Beginners may prefer the left fork (Road 8303), with several miles of nearly level skiing west into the Cougar Creek drainage. However, for the best views take the right fork, climbing continually. If you stay right at all major intersections you may ski for 2½ more miles to a 3700-foot high point at the northern end of the ridge and front-row views of the volcano.

81 MOUNT ST. HELENS

Skill level: mountaineer
Round trip: 8 miles
Skiing time: 6 hours
Elevation gain: 4665 feet
High point: 8365 feet

Best: January–May
Avalanche potential: moderate
Map: Green Trails, Mount St.
*   Helens Northwest*

The popular saying of 1980, "Don't come to Washington, let Washington come to you," aptly describes how the upper 1300 feet of Mount St. Helens spread themselves over the neighboring states. Times have changed, and since the Forest Service reopened the mountain in 1987, throngs of onlookers have paid a visit to this lunar landscape.

Many of the visitors bring skis because the mountain has lowered itself to very skiable proportions. In fact, the energetic can ski it twice in a day. The slopes are fairly uniform and when the sun softens the snow they are skiable by any competent kick-turner.

But skiing Mount St. Helens isn't a cakewalk. When the snows refuse to soften, the icy slopes are a horror to three-pinners, and nasty, even fatal slides are possible. In addition there are dangers to skiing any major

Open slopes below Monitor Ridge

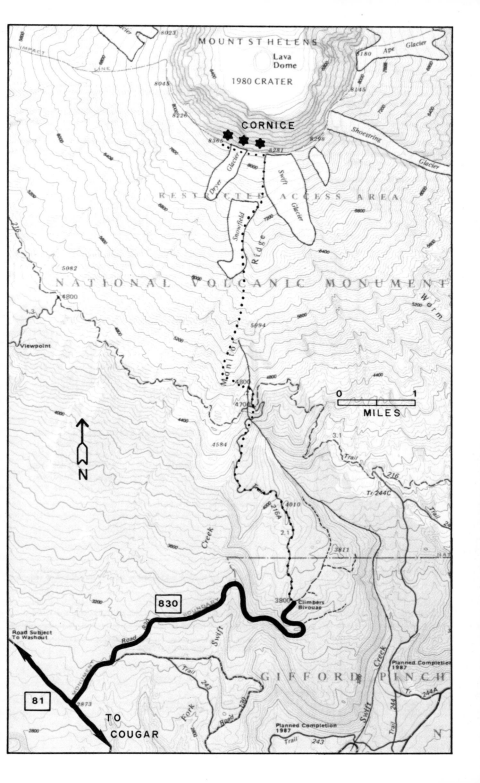

peak, especially an active volcano, that demand the skill and judgment of experienced mountaineers.

Skiing above 4800 feet on Mount St. Helens requires a permit. An unlimited number of these permits are issued daily between November 1 and May 15 at the Yale Park climbing register. From May 16 through October, however, only 100 permits are issued per day—70 of these permits may be reserved in advance by writing to Mount St. Helens Volcanic National Monument Headquarters, Route 1, Box 269, Amboy, Washington 98601. The remaining 30 permits are available at Yale Park on a first-come first-served basis on the day of the tour. When volcanic hazard is high, no permits are issued.

Access: Exit Interstate 5 at Woodland and drive east toward Cougar to Yale Park and register. Drive on 9 miles, passing through Cougar to an intersection. Turn left on Forest Road 83 and drive 3 miles before turning left on Forest Road 81. When the snow level is low, park at the junction of Roads 83 and 81. (A Sno-Park permit is required.) Conditions allowing, drive up Forest Road 81 for 1.7 miles, then go right on spur road 830, which is followed for 2.7 steep miles up to an informal dry camping area known as the Climbers Bivouac (3700 feet). Several unmarked roads will be passed on the way up. To stay on Road 830, always remain on the road that climbs.

The Tour: From the Climbers Bivouac follow the Ptarmigan Trail, No. 216A, to timberline. Once out of the trees turn right and follow a gully up to a small bench (4800 feet) where the real climb begins. Ski west, climbing a steepish slope to the ridge top, then head north toward the crater rim, skiing up a series of narrow gullies and ribs on the west side of Monitor Ridge. At 6200 feet the last gully peters out and a steep (often icy) slope must be cautiously traversed or avoided by dropping below it. When the snow is unstable the slope should be completely avoided by climbing to the ridge above and following the exposed rocks to the main snow slopes.

Once the steep slope is traversed, climb to the right (east), following the natural roll of the terrain up Monitor Ridge to the crest at 7200 feet. On the left, skirt a large bowl, which is prone to avalanche when the snow is unstable. Once on the ridge, turn north and ski the open slopes toward the crater. Near the 8281-foot summit *stop* a good 20 feet before the rim, completely avoiding the *huge* and *extremely dangerous* cornices that hang over the crater and tempt the suicidal to step nearer. Mark our words: a few poor suckers are going to bite the big one when their weight combined with sunshine or a little tremor causes one of those monsters to let loose. Don't let it be you. If you want to look in the crater, traverse west along the rim and find an area where the snow has melted down to the pumice.

The true summit (8365) lies about ¼ mile to the west and is rarely visited. To reach it, descend at least 100 feet and traverse, staying well away from the edge of the crater.

Be sure and sign out at Yale Park on the way home.

Ascending along Monitor Ridge, Mount Hood in distance

Forest near Red Rock Pass

82 RED ROCK PASS

Skill level: *advanced basic*
Round trip: *5 miles*
Skiing time: *3 hours*
Elevation gain: *860 feet*
High point: *3100 feet*

Best: *January–February*
Avalanche potential: *none*
Map: *Green Trails, Mount St.
Helens*

Map on page 202

Open meadows, views to the steaming crater rim, roads, and trails are all elements of this tour along the southwestern base of Mount St. Helens. This is an excellent half- or whole-day trip with excellent campsite locations for anyone wishing to camp out.

Access: Take the Woodland exit off Interstate 5 and drive State Route 503 east to Cougar. Go straight through Cougar and continue east for another 6.8 miles. Turn left on Forest Road 83 and drive north until the road divides at 2.7 miles. Go left on Road 81, which immediately ends at a small Sno-Park (2240 feet).

The Tour: Head up trampled Road 81 with skiers, climbers, and a few very noisy snowmobiles for company. The road climbs steadily for the first 1½ miles through forest with an occasional view over the hillsides to the south for thrills.

Road 830 branches off on the right at 1½ miles, marking a change in the topography. The forest opens and you are treated to meadows topped by views of Mount St. Helens. There are forests of ghost trees, killed by mud slides. To the south are more meadows and views of seemingly endless hills.

Near 2½ miles the road crosses narrow Red Rock Pass which funnels the east and west winds to make it the windiest spot in the area. On the right (north) side of the pass is the Toutle River Trail, the best destination for skiers looking for quiet campsites or picnic spots away from the snowmobiles. The trail starts with a steep 30-foot climb up the bank at the edge of the road, then levels out, heading due northwest through light forest and meadows.

You may stay on Road 81 and descend for a mile to an overlook of McBride Lake, then continue down to cross the Kalama River to reach the meadows and swamps of the Kalama Springs area (there are good campsites here, also). If you are lucky you may spot one of the elk that winter around the lake in the spring. If you fail to spot the animals themselves, you will probably see at least one elk trail trampled deep into the snow.

83 JUNE LAKE LOOP

June Lake

Skill level: advanced basic
Round trip: 5 miles
Skiing time: 3 hours
Elevation gain: 460 feet
High point: 3100 feet
Best: January–February
Avalanche potential: none
Map: Green Trails, Mount
  St. Helens

The Loop

Skill level: intermediate
Round trip: 5 miles
Skiing time: 3 hours
Elevation gain: 560 feet
High point: 3200 feet
Best: January–February
Avalanche potential: low
Map: Green Trails, Mount
  St. Helens

Map on page 202

June Lake Loop is a four-star tour reached by a trail designed for skiers. There is a lake, waterfall, unlimited views of snow-covered Mount St. Helens, sheltered campsites, and a loop for those inclined.

Access: Exit Interstate 5 at Woodland and drive east on State Route 503 for 28.8 miles to Cougar. Go straight through town and continue east for another 6.8 miles, then turn left on Forest Road 83. In 3 miles the road divides; stay right on Road 83 for another 2.7 miles to the Sno-Park at the end of the plowing (2640 feet).

The Tour: The Sno-Park lies at the intersection of Road 8312 (Marble Mountain, Tour 84) and Road 83. Start your tour by skiing the left fork (Road 83) on a surface packed hard by snowmobiles and skis. The road is nearly level for the first 1½ miles to the June Lake turnoff.

As you ski along Road 83 you will pass several roads branching off to the left. At ¼ mile from the Sno-Park glide pass the Swift Creek Skier Trail, the return route for loopers. June Lake Skier Trail is the fourth road on the left, starting 1 mile from the Sno-Park.

The trail heads up an old clearcut first on road then on a broad, well-marked trail. Ahead Mount St. Helens is in full view. At 2½ miles from the Sno-Park enter the Mount St. Helens National Volcanic Monument just as the trail makes a short, steep drop to a small logging platform. There is a short climb followed by a bridge, then you ski out onto an open bench. June Lake and the waterfall are to your right, bounded by steep cliffs (3100 feet). The level area near the lake offers excellent campsites. Stay back from the edge of the lake, as it is difficult to determine where the lakeshore starts in this broad, flat field of snow.

Skiers opting to make the loop should climb the open slope beyond the lake, heading toward the mountain. (Most years this route is marked by flags.) Near the top of the slope go left and ski down to a small wooded

Bridge near June Lake

bench (good campsites). Cross the bench and climb up and over a steep rib, angling toward the mountain.

At ½ mile from June Lake is the Swift Creek Skier Trail, a narrow corridor through the forest well marked with orange tape and blue diamonds. Go left and descend the down along Swift Creek back to Road 83. Here you will turn right and ski ¼ mile back to the Sno-Park to close the loop.

84 MARBLE MOUNTAIN

Skill level: advanced basic
Round trip: 11 miles
Skiing time: 6 hours
Elevation gain: 1488 feet
High point: 4128 feet
Best: January–mid-March

Avalanche potential: low
Map: Green Trails, Mount St.
  Helens

Map on page 202

A full day of views and a delightful tour await all skiers willing to brave the snowmobiles on Marble Mountain.

Access: Drive to the upper Sno-Park on Forest Road 83 and park (2640 feet; see Tour 83 for directions).

The Tour: The Sno-Park is located at the intersection of Road 83 and Road 8312. Start your tour by skiing down the right fork (Road 8312), descending gradually for the first ¼ mile to a snow-covered swamp. However, before you have time to really get into good downhill form, the road levels, crosses a small stream, and at ¾ mile starts to climb.

The climb is steady to the south, traversing into a small side valley, then abruptly turning east to open slopes. Starting at 2 miles are tremendous views of the south side of Mount St. Helens from the crater rim down the gleaming white slopes, through the Worm Flows formations to the forest below.

At 2¾ miles (3340 feet), cross through a shallow pass and head southeast over broad, rolling clearcut slopes. Here the road levels and it's time to practice skating on the snowmobile-packed surface. There are several side roads in this section; however, with Marble Mountain straight ahead you are unlikely to stray.

The road starts to climb again near 4¼ miles, wrapping its way to the 4128-foot summit of Marble Mountain and views of Mount Adams, Swift Reservoir, endless clearcuts, roads, and forests. (On a clear day you may prefer to cut a mile or two from the total by leaving Road 8312 near mile 3 and skiing due east to the summit.)

Snomobiles are in evidence on this road nearly every day. Although the road is too short for the machines to get in a full day's exercise, the open meadows above the 3-mile point draw them in. Start your trip early, but not too early to miss their antics as they turn around in the limited space found at the summit. If you feel that snowmobiles do not belong on this road, please add your letter to ours and write: District Ranger, Mount St. Helens National Volcanic Monument, Amboy, WA 98601.

Open slopes on Marble Mountain

AND MORE SKI TOURS

The 84 ski tours covered by this book barely scratch the surface of the skiing opportunities in the South Cascades and Olympics. Following is a listing of other places to explore. Unless otherwise noted, these tours are suggested for advanced basic or intermediate skiers.

Keechelus Lake

Source Lake–Snow Lake: Extreme avalanche potential. Area not recommended for winter travel.

Commonwealth Basin: Good access to basin by Pacific Crest Trail or straight up the hillside on an old trail route. High avalanche potential from the edge of the timber above the basin and on up.

Cle Elum Lake

Corral Creek Loop: Groomed snowmobile loop. Ski on weekdays to avoid the machines. Starts on Forest Road 4305 (see Hex Mountain, Tour 23).

Lake Tucquala (Fish Lake): A 15-mile road ski to snowbound lake. Heavy snowmobile use. Drive to end of plowed road at Salmon la Sac and ski up main road.

Swauk Creek

Cougar Gulch: Ski Road 9718 to open meadows and excellent viewpoints; can be joined with Road 9712 to form a loop. Area receives heavy snowmobile use, so best skied midweek. Access, take the Liberty turnoff from Highway 97 and drive north of the town.

Lion Gulch: Ski Road 9712 to open meadows with excellent views of Mount Rainier. This is a snowmobile area and best skied midweek. Access, take the Liberty turnoff from Highway 97 and drive to the south end of town.

Blue Creek: A 15-mile round trip on road leads to open ridge tops and views. Ski up Road 9738 and go left on Road 9702 to reach the base of Red Top Mountain Lookout. Access, see Tour 32.

Pipe Creek Road: No machines are allowed on this three-pronged road. Spur Road 141 divides; the left fork goes 1½ miles up to Swauk Pass, the right fork climbs 1½ miles to Swauk Meadows, and Spur Road 140 climbs up Pipe Creek for 2½ miles to views of the Stuart Range. Access, 2 miles south of Swauk Pass on Highway 97.

Scotty Creek: An 8-mile road ski. Some snowmobile use. Access from the north-side Swauk Pass Sno-Park.

Table Mountain: Miles of road and open country to explore. Area receives heavy snowmobile use. Access to Table Mountain (Tour 38).

White River

Grass Mountain: Excellent views from Grass Mountain Lookout and good skiing on the open ridge tops. Access, turn left off Highway 410 on a private logging road 6 miles east of the Mud Mountain Dam road.

West Fork White River: Spring skiing and excellent views from roads and clearcuts on Frog Mountain once West Fork Road is open. Access, 3 miles south of the town of Greenwater on Highway 410.

Dalles Ridge: Miles of logging roads to explore and clearcut slopes for telemarking. Area receives heavy snowmobile use. Access: 2 miles south of the town of Greenwater, turn left off Highway 410 onto Road 70. Drive east to Road 72.

Greenwater Road: A 10-mile road ski to Government Meadows. Considerable snowmobile use. Access, 2 miles south of Greenwater on Highway 410.

Silver Springs Sno-Park: Marked ski trail along the White River. Access: see Tour 45.

Naches River

Nile Creek Road: Best: for early- or late-season skiing when the road is open as far as feed station. Destination and miles variable. Access is from Highway 410 at town of Nile.

Cougar Valley: Long road approach to magnificent views. Best for early- or late-season skiing when Road 1902 is open to upper Sand Creek Trailhead. Access is from Little Naches River Road.

American River

Blankenship Meadows: A 7-mile trail ski to meadows and lakes below Tumac Mountain for advanced skiers. Access is from Bumping Lake (Tour 51). Tour starts by skiing around the west side of the lake.

Mount Rainier

Nisqually Vista: A ¾-mile round trip on marked trail. Good views of mountain and glacier. Rated easiest by the Park Service but very steep in sections. Access, trail starts behind Paradise Visitor Center.

Sunrise: No parking until the park-entrance road has melted out as far as the White River Bridge, generally late May or June. Ski 10 miles to end of road then out on open, rolling Burroughs Mountain. Excellent views of Mount Rainier.

Randle Area

Strawberry Mountain Sno-Park: Sno-Park should be in place by the winter of 1988. There will be roads and trails reserved for self-propelled use as well as access to the open ridge tops and telemark slopes; good views of Mount St. Helens. Access from Randle on Road 25 to Road 99.

Orr Creek: Marked trail for skiers. Access, see Tour 65. Trail starts from the Sno-Park.

Pimlico Creek: East access to the Hamilton Buttes area. Best skied in spring when Road 21 is open to Cat Creek. Access, see Tour 64.

Tieton River

Leech Lake: Nine miles of groomed ski trails on the north side of White Pass. Part of the White Pass Ski Area concession; a fee is charged.

North Fork Tieton River: A skier-only road, good for first-time skiers. For access, see Tour 70 for driving directions.

Olympics

Hamma Hamma River Road: Low-elevation valley-bottom tour. As much as 10 miles of skiable road each way. Access is from Highway 101, 2 miles north of Eldon.

Dosewallips River Road: Low-elevation valley-bottom skiing past falls to road-end (5 to 10 miles from snowline). Access off Highway 101 just north of Dosewallips State Park.

Hoh River Trail: Advanced skiers may ski a low-elevation valley-bottom trail 8 miles to Olympus Shelter. Trail through rain forest and, if lucky, past herds of elk. Access trail starts at Hoh River Visitor Center.

Columbia River

Sasquatch Trail: Trail marked for self-propelled users, with outstanding view of Mount St. Helens. Access, see Tour 83.

TRAILS CLASSIFIED BY USE

Multiple Use

1. Bessemer Mountain
2. Milwaukee Railroad Grade
3. Bandera Overlook
4. Hansen Creek
7. Mount Margaret
8. Flatlanders' Route on Keechelus Ridge
9. Relay Tower–Keechelus Ridge
10. That Dam Loop
11. Another Lost Lake
12. Yakima Valley Overview
13. The Dandy Loops
14. Stampede Pass
15. Kachess Lake Campground
16. Swan Lake
17. Amabilis Mountain
20. More Cabin Creek
22. Wenatchee Mountains
23. Hex Mountain
24. French Cabin Creek
25. Cle Elum River
26. Jolly and Jolly Too
27. Jolly Mountain
28. Pete Lake and Cooper Pass
29. Cooper River Trail
30. Teanaway Butte
31. Teanaway River and Bean Creek Basin
32. Red Top Mountain Lookover
33. Iron Creek
34. Blewett Pass
35. Hurley Creek Loop
37. Wenatchee Ridge
39. Whistler Creek
40. Twin Camp
41. Huckleberry Ridge
43. Grand Park
45. Corral Pass
50. Almost a Loop of Bumping Lake
51. Miners Ridge

52. Manastash Ridge
53. Rocky Prairie
60. Copper Creek Road
61. High Rock View
62. Lookout Mountain
63. Burley Mountain
64. Hamilton Buttes
65. Green Mountain
66. Snyder Mountain Loop
71. Lost Lake
72. Bear Canyon
73. The Elk Tour
74. Mount Washington
75. Four Stream Road
76. Mount Townsend
82. Red Rock Pass
84. Marble Mountain

Groomed Ski Trail

5. Snoqualmie Pass—Tracked and Untracked

Self-Propelled

6. Kendall—Knobs, Lakes, and Loops
18. Cabin Creek
19. South Kachess Lake
21. John Wayne Trail
36. Swauk Pass Loops
38. Haney Meadow
42. Sun Top Lookout
44. Buck Creek Tour
46. Norse Peak
47. Silver Basin
48. Chinook Pass and Naches Peak
49. Pleasant Valley Loop
54. Mowich Lake
55. Seattle Park and Russell Glacier
56. Reflection Lakes
57. Tatoosh Range
58. Mazama Ridge

SUGGESTED READING

Avalanche Safety

Fraser, Colin. *Avalanches and Snow Safety.* New York: Charles Scribner's Sons, 1978.

LaChappelle, E. R. *The ABC of Avalanche Safety,* 2nd ed. Seattle: The Mountaineers, 1985.

Peters, Ed, ed. *Mountaineering: The Freedom of the Hills.* 4th ed. Seattle: The Mountaineers, 1982.

Enjoying the Outdoors (Proper clothing, ski equipment, winter camping)

Brady, Michael. *Cross-Country Ski Gear,* 2nd ed. Seattle: The Mountaineers, 1988.

Tejada-Flores, Lito. *Backcountry Skiing.* San Francisco: Sierra Club Books, 1981.

Watters, Ron. *Ski Camping.* San Francisco: Chronicle Books, 1979.

How To

Barnett, Steve. *Cross-Country Downhill.* 2nd ed. Seattle: Pacific Search Press, 1979.

Bein, Vic. *Mountain Skiing.* Seattle: The Mountaineers, 1982.

Gillette, Ned, and Dostal, John. *Cross-Country Skiing.* 3rd ed. Seattle: The Mountaineers, 1988.

First Aid

Lentz, Martha; Macdonald, Steven; and Carline, Jan. *Mountaineering First Aid.* 3rd ed. Seattle: The Mountaineers, 1985.

Wilkerson, James A., M.D., ed. *Medicine for Mountaineering.* 3rd ed. Seattle: The Mountaineers, 1985.

INDEX

About the authors:

Tom Kirkendall and Vicky Spring, residents of Edmonds, Washington, are both experienced outdoor people and enthusiastic skiers. The couple travel the hills in summer as hikers, backpackers and cyclists on mountain bikes; when the snow falls, they pin on cross-country skis and keep on exploring. Both Vicky and Tom studied at the Brooks Institute of Photography in Santa Barbara, California, and are now building their careers together as outdoor photographers and guidebook authors. Vicky (who first stood up on skis at age three) had something of a head start in the field, beginning in the days when she carried a backpack of camera gear for her well-known outdoor photographer father, Ira Spring.

Vicky and Tom are the authors of *Bicycling the Pacific Coast,* and *Cross-Country Ski Trails of Washington's Cascades and Olympics;* she is co-author and photographer of *94 Hikes* and *95 Hikes in the Canadian Rockies;* and he is author/photographer of *Mountain Bike Adventures in Washington's North Cascades & Olympics* and *in Washington's South Cascades & Puget Sound,* all published by The Mountaineers.

Other books from The Mountaineers include:

BACKCOUNTRY SKIING in Washington's Cascades, Rainer Burgdorfer
Detailed guidebook to 78 backcountry tours for intermediate, advanced
ski-mountaineers.

CROSS-COUNTRY SKI ROUTES of Oregon's Cascades, Klindt Vielbig
Details and maps on 197 tours, loops and connector links, for skiers from
beginning to intermediate, for Mt. Hood, Bend areas.

ABC OF AVALANCHE SAFETY, 2nd Ed., Ed LaChapelle
Classic handbook on basics of avalanches — determining potential areas,
traveling in avalanche terrain, reactions if caught, search, rescue.

COLORADO HIGH ROUTES: Aspen-Vail-Crested Butte Ski Tours Including the
Tenth Mountain Trail, Louis W. Dawson
Detailed guide to over 95 ski-mountaineering routes, from beginner-
intermediate to advanced.

CROSS-COUNTRY SKIING, 3rd Ed., Ned Gillette, John Dostal
Zany and instructive how-to information on skiing everything from track to
backcountry, by two experts.

CROSS-COUNTRY SKI GEAR, Michael Brady
Latest information on materials, design and construction techniques and
how choice affects skiing performance.

HYPOTHERMIA, FROSTBITE AND OTHER COLD INJURIES: Prevention,
Recognition, Prehospital Treatment, Wilkerson, Bangs, Hayward
Medical experts describe hypothermia's effects on the body, how to
avoid it, how to recognize signs and how to treat it; includes frostbite
and immersion.

SNOWSHOEING, 3rd Ed., Prater
Latest information about equipment and techniques for varying terrain
and snow conditions.

Ask for illustrated catalog of more than 150 outdoor titles:

The Mountaineers
306 Second Avenue West, Seattle WA 98119
(206) 285-2665
Order toll-free 1-800-553-4453